Acting Edition

The Keen Collection Volume 10

Buck Stars
by C. Julian Jiménez

**Kirdle & Miffins:
Curiosity Saved the Cats**
Book, Music & Lyrics
by Rona Siddiqui

Hidden Inside
by Daniel Carlton and Nambi E. Kelley

SAMUEL FRENCH

Buck Stars © 2024 by C. Julian Jiménez
Kirdle & Miffins: Curiosity Saved the Cats © 2024 by Rona Siddiqui
Hidden Inside © 2024 by Daniel Carlton and Nambi E. Kelley
All Rights Reserved

THE KEEN COLLECTION: VOLUME 10 is fully protected under the copyright laws of the United States of America, the British Commonwealth, including Canada, and all member countries of the Berne Convention for the Protection of Literary and Artistic Works, the Universal Copyright Convention, and/or the World Trade Organization conforming to the Agreement on Trade Related Aspects of Intellectual Property Rights. All rights, including professional and amateur stage productions, recitation, lecturing, public reading, motion picture, radio broadcasting, television, online/digital production, and the rights of translation into foreign languages are strictly reserved.

ISBN 978-0-573-71108-4

www.concordtheatricals.com
www.concordtheatricals.co.uk

FOR PRODUCTION INQUIRIES

UNITED STATES AND CANADA
info@concordtheatricals.com
1-866-979-0447

UNITED KINGDOM AND EUROPE
licensing@concordtheatricals.co.uk
020-7054-7298

Each title is subject to availability from Concord Theatricals Corp., depending upon country of performance. Please be aware that *THE KEEN COLLECTION: VOLUME 10* may not be licensed by Concord Theatricals Corp. in your territory. Professional and amateur producers should contact the nearest Concord Theatricals Corp. office or licensing partner to verify availability.

CAUTION: Professional and amateur producers are hereby warned that *THE KEEN COLLECTION: VOLUME 10* is subject to a licensing fee. The purchase, renting, lending or use of this book does not constitute a license to perform this title(s), which license must be obtained from Concord Theatricals Corp. prior to any performance. Performance of this title(s) without a license is a violation of federal law and may subject the producer and/or presenter of such performances to civil penalties. Both amateurs and professionals considering a production are strongly advised to apply to the appropriate agent before starting rehearsals, advertising, or booking a theatre. A licensing fee must be paid whether the title(s) is presented for charity or gain and whether or not admission is charged. Professional/Stock licensing fees are quoted upon application to Concord Theatricals Corp.

This work is published by Samuel French, an imprint of Concord Theatricals Corp.

No one shall make any changes in this title(s) for the purpose of production. No part of this book may be reproduced, stored in a retrieval system, scanned, uploaded, or transmitted in any form, by any means, now known or yet to be invented, including mechanical, electronic, digital, photocopying, recording, videotaping, or otherwise, without the prior written permission of the publisher. No one shall share this title(s), or any part of this title(s), through any social media or file hosting websites.

For all inquiries regarding motion picture, television, online/digital and other media rights, please contact Concord Theatricals Corp.

MUSIC AND THIRD-PARTY MATERIALS USE NOTE

Licensees are solely responsible for obtaining formal written permission from copyright owners to use copyrighted music and/or other copyrighted third-party materials (e.g. artworks, logos) in the performance of this play and are strongly cautioned to do so. If no such permission is obtained by the licensee, then the licensee must use only original music and materials that the licensee owns and controls. Licensees are solely responsible and liable for clearances of all third-party copyrighted materials, including without limitation music, and shall indemnify the copyright owners of the play(s) and their licensing agent, Concord Theatricals Corp., against any costs, expenses, losses and liabilities arising from the use of such copyrighted third-party materials by licensees. For music, please contact the appropriate music licensing authority in your territory for the rights to any incidental music.

IMPORTANT BILLING AND CREDIT REQUIREMENTS

If you have obtained performance rights to this title, please refer to your licensing agreement for important billing and credit requirements.

TABLE OF CONTENTS

About Keen Teens vii

Keen Teens Ambassadors................................ ix

Buck Stars 1

Kirdle & Miffins: Curiosity Saved the Cats...................27

Hidden Inside...63

ABOUT KEEN TEENS

Founded in 2000, Keen Company is an award-winning Off-Broadway theatre producing stories about the decisive moments that change us. Central to Keen Company's mission is to present theatre that patrons can identify with and connect to. The Keen Teens program is the cornerstone of the company's outreach and educational efforts, bringing the company's values to the high school stage by developing new work tailored specifically to teen actors and audiences.

When first creating Keen Teens in 2007, the company found that teachers did not have access to material intended for a high school stage. Educators were left to present either classic plays never designed for teen actors, or material created specifically for school groups that lacked richness or relevance. Through Keen Teens, the company began commissioning original plays and musicals that are as complex and multilayered as the lives of high school students today, penned by accomplished professional playwrights and musical theatre writers.

There are two components to Keen Teens: The first is a free program for New York City-area high school students to work alongside professional writers, directors, and designers to rehearse and premiere these plays Off-Broadway. The second is that the plays then go on to be published and licensed through our partners at Concord Theatricals as *The Keen Collection*.

The Keen Collection is made up of comedies, dramas, and musicals; scripts range from the sincere to the absurd, from the existential to the most intimate. Some deal head-on with topical issues, others simply aim to provide smart, contemporary material. These original pieces have been created by many of the most talented writers working today, including Bekah Brunstetter, Kristoffer Diaz, Madeleine George, C.A. Johnson, Greg Kotis, Mike Lew, James Tyler, Leah Nanako Winkler, and Lauren Yee. This group includes finalists for the Pulitzer, Wendy Wasserstein, and Susan Smith Blackburn Prizes; and winners of the Yale Drama Series Prize, Horton Foote Playwriting Award, and more. Their theatrical work has been produced professionally on and Off-Broadway, and their writing has reached an international audience on TV shows including *Girls*, *GLOW*, *Mad Men*, *Mozart in the Jungle*, *Nurse Jackie*, *Tales of the City*, and *This Is Us*.

As well as being tailored to the social and emotional world of teens, these plays are also designed to be accessible in educational settings. All scripts run thirty minutes, with simple design elements, large ensembles, and flexible casting requirements. Each play can be presented on its own or in combination with other *Keen Collection* titles on a shared bill.

Keen Teens has made possible the Off-Broadway debut of over three hundred young actors and has led to the publication of over thirty-five new one-act plays and musicals, which are regularly produced not only in the United States, but in countries around the world, from Australia to Singapore.

For more information, please visit www.keencompany.org/keenteens.

Keen Teens Staff

Celestine Rae, *Education Director*
Ashley Scott, *Associate Producer*
Jeremy Stoller, *Director of New Work*

Keen Company Staff

Jonathan Silverstein, *Artistic Director*
Ashley DiGiorgi, *Managing Producer*
Reed Ridgley, *General Manager*
Brad Ogden, *Marketing Manager*

KEEN TEENS AMBASSADORS

Keen Teens is made possible with the support of our Keen Teens Ambassadors:

The Axe-Houghton Foundation
The Marta Heflin Foundation
Lauren Bakoian
Jeff Becker
Stephanie Bok
Bill and Casey Bradford
Maria Brause
Paul Brill
Kyle Cardone
Kathleen and Henry Chalfant
Elizabeth Corradino
Rose Courtney
Alexander Cox
Bill Craco
Linda D'Onofrio
Michaela Daliana
Robert Donnalley
  and Joan Weingarten
Amyt Eckstein
David Esbjornson
Kelsey Farrell
Amy Glass
Barbara Gottlieb
Timothy Grandia
Mike Griot
Bao Ho
Sally Humphreys
Sally and Robert Huxley
Frank Iryami
Jon Isler
Hattie Jutagir
Robert and Nina Kaufelt
Charles MacLeod
Emily MacLeod
Jeremiah Maestas
Liz and Rafi Magnes
Oren Mandel
Marsha Mason
Cynthia and Bruce Miltenberg
Carl Monte
Deirdre O'Connell
Caroline Palmer
David and Faith Pedowitz
Katherine and David Rabinowitz
Kayam Rajaram
M. Kilburg Reedy
Kitab Rollins
Michael Rose and Heidi Hoover
Courtney Renee Sargent
Matt Servitto
Nisha Sheth
Alice Silkworth
Lisa Soeder
Olga Staffen
Jillian Steadman
Marjolein Steenbergen
Randy Strickland
Pearl Sun
Dan Swern
Stephanie Swirsky
Pamela Thomas
Jen VanDemark
Sarah Wells
Aulene Wessel
Emily Wexler
Kara Winslow
Pia Winslow
Marie Wolpert
Emmy Zuckerman and Ed Bonfield

Buck Stars

by C. Julian Jiménez

BUCK STARS premiered with Keen Company (Jonathan Silverstein, Artistic Director) as part of the Keen Teens Festival of New Work (Celestine Rae, Festival Artistic Director) at Theatre Row in New York City on May 19, 2023. The performance was directed by Michelle Chan, with sets by Indigo Shea, costumes by Brittani Beresford, lights by Alex DeNevers, and sound by Jordana Abrenica. The Production Stage Manager was Sloane Fischer. The cast was as follows:

COLLEGE STUDENT	Kaleb Joseph
TABLE HOG	Kyla Jones
LOOKING	Xavier Gonzalez
FIRST GEN	Lesly Montano
DOWN LOW	Dereck Diller
UNSHELTERED	Bianca Vigilante
MANAGER	Sunam Govind
CASHIER	Mi'kayla Bracero
BARISTA	Annahlyn Barrett
APPLICANT	Ellie Altebrando

CHARACTERS

COLLEGE STUDENT – (any gender/ethnicity) Resents useless college classes.

TABLE HOG – (any gender/ethnicity) Resents their day job.

LOOKING – (male/any ethnicity) Resents modern dating.

FIRST GEN – (any gender/first generation immigrant) Resents the privileged.

DOWN LOW – (male/any ethnicity) Resents their life.

UNSHELTERED – (any gender/ethnicity) Resents not having a job.

MANAGER – (any gender/ethnicity) Resents the lack of pride people have for their job.

CASHIER – (any gender/ethnicity) Resents their dependence on substance to do their job.

BARISTA – (any gender/ethnicity) Resents that health benefits are dependent on a dead-end job.

APPLICANT – (female/any ethnicity) Resents having to get a job.

AUTHOR'S NOTES

The character of **FIRST GEN** can be played by any first-generation immigrant actor. First-generation immigrants are the first foreign-born family members to gain citizenship or permanent residency in the United States. Any Spanish in the script can be replaced with a language that corresponds to the actor playing **FIRST GEN**.

*(We are at a corporate coffeehouse chain. The chain shouldn't be literal but should be easily recognizable as a corporate coffeehouse chain with a few costume or prop elements. Maybe a stack of coffee cups? Perhaps **CASHIER** and **BARISTA** don a green apron? Some half and half containers?)*

(The scene moves from conversation to conversation – thought to thought.)

(A bell on the front door rings.)

*(**COLLEGE STUDENT** enters.)*

*(**TABLE HOG** follows behind.)*

(They both are rushing to claim a table near an outlet.)

*(**TABLE HOG** is behind but then throws their messenger bag over **COLLEGE STUDENT**'s head onto the table.)*

(They face off.)

*(**TABLE HOG** sits at the table they have claimed with their bag.)*

*(**COLLEGE STUDENT** snaps their fingers. Lights shift. Everyone freezes.)*

COLLEGE STUDENT. *(To audience.)* I walk into a crowded Starbucks and try to claim a table. My MacBook is at forty-percent battery. I've got a paper due on *Beowulf* tomorrow so I'm gonna need the power. Things at home are always a bit frantic, so the white noise of a public coffeehouse is basically as serene as the crashing of ocean waves.

But nothing says public coffeehouse like table hogs like this one, who will keep asking for refills of hot water for their lifeless tea bag while they sit here for the next six hours. I guess I'll sit here in the meantime and stalk out a table with an outlet.

> (**COLLEGE STUDENT** *sits at a table and snaps their fingers. Lights shift. Everyone unfreezes.*)
>
> (**COLLEGE STUDENT** *sees* **LOOKING** *wrap up their phone charger.* **COLLEGE STUDENT** *throws their bag over to* **LOOKING**'s *table.*)

LOOKING. Down Low?

COLLEGE STUDENT. I'm sorry?

LOOKING. Your handle? Are you Down Low?

COLLEGE STUDENT. No.

LOOKING. Just up and high, huh?

COLLEGE STUDENT. Are you leaving?

LOOKING. Maybe. Are you leaving?

COLLEGE STUDENT. I need a charge.

LOOKING. You get right to the point.

COLLEGE STUDENT. An outlet. I need an outlet.

LOOKING. Don't we all, honey.

> (**COLLEGE STUDENT** *snaps their fingers. Lights shift. Everyone freezes.*)

COLLEGE STUDENT. *(To audience.)* I think he's hitting on me.

(**COLLEGE STUDENT** *snaps their fingers. Lights shift. Everyone unfreezes.*)

Can I have your table?

LOOKING. You can have much more than that.

(**COLLEGE STUDENT** *snaps their fingers. Lights shift. Everyone freezes.*)

COLLEGE STUDENT. *(To audience.)* He's definitely hitting on me.

LOOKING. *(To audience.)* It's hard to know who you'll actually end up meeting when all you've seen is a pic of a headless torso courtesy of the gay guillotine. Sometimes the profile pic is a landscape…or a pixelated meme. These hookup apps are…well…kind of a hellscape.

(**LOOKING** *snaps their fingers. Light shift. Everyone unfreezes.*)

It's all yours.

COLLEGE STUDENT. Thanks.

(**LOOKING** *doesn't move.*)

Wait. What's all mine?

(**LOOKING** *snaps their fingers. Lights shift. Everyone freezes.*)

(**LOOKING** *sighs audibly to the audience.*)

(**LOOKING** *snaps their fingers. Lights shift. Everyone unfreezes.*)

LOOKING. The outlet.

COLLEGE STUDENT. Cool beans.

LOOKING. Is that a coffee joke?

COLLEGE STUDENT. Huh?

(**LOOKING** *leaves the table.*)

(**COLLEGE STUDENT** *plugs in their laptop. They look around and see* **FIRST GEN** *sitting close by.*)

(*To* **FIRST GEN.**) Can you watch my things while I order my drink?

FIRST GEN. (*In foreign language.*) Qué, soy tu guardia? (*Do I look like your security guard?*)

(**COLLEGE STUDENT** *snaps their fingers. Lights shift. Everyone freezes.*)

COLLEGE STUDENT. (*To audience.*) Foreign.

FIRST GEN. (*To audience.*) I tried speaking in my native tongue to avoid watching this loser's crap, but Americans love their outlets.

(**FIRST GEN** *snaps their fingers. Lights shift. Everyone unfreezes.*)

COLLEGE STUDENT. CAN. YOU. WATCH. MY. STUFF?

(**FIRST GEN** *nods.*)

(**COLLEGE STUDENT** *walks over to the counter.*)

(**FIRST GEN** *snaps their fingers. Lights shift. Everyone freezes.*)

FIRST GEN. (*To audience.*) They think the louder they speak, the more I understand…when actually, I don't care. I know English well, but I refuse to give them the satisfaction.

(*Beat.*)

Stupid Americans.

(**FIRST GEN** *snaps their fingers. Lights shift. Everyone unfreezes.*)

(A bell on the front door rings.)

(**DOWN LOW** *walks in and sees* **LOOKING**.)

LOOKING. Down Low?

DOWN LOW. I'm sorry?

LOOKING. Your handle? Are you Down Low?

(**LOOKING** *points to himself in an attempt at clarity.*)

Looking25.

(**DOWN LOW** *snaps their fingers. Lights shift. Everyone freezes.*)

DOWN LOW. *(To audience.)* He looks just like his photo on Grindr. I wasn't expecting that. I heard to always expect older.

(**DOWN LOW** *snaps their fingers. Lights shift. Everyone unfreezes.*)

Hi.

LOOKING. Hello.

DOWN LOW. Hi.

(**LOOKING** *snaps their fingers. Lights shift. Everyone freezes.*)

LOOKING. This is why I usually avoid guys on the DL. It's always so tedious and makes a hookup require way more effort than they need to.

DOWN LOW. *(To audience.)* What if someone recognizes me?

LOOKING. *(To audience.)* I hope someone recognizes him.

DOWN LOW. *(To audience.)* My God. He's gorgeous.

> (**DOWN LOW** *snaps their fingers. Lights shift. Everyone unfreezes.*)

Can I get you a latte?

LOOKING. I'm not really interested in coffee right now.

DOWN LOW. Tea?

LOOKING. Here I am. In a public place. Can we go somewhere private now?

DOWN LOW. Can we talk for a bit?

LOOKING. Talk?

> (**LOOKING** *snaps their fingers. Lights shift. Everyone freezes.*)

(To audience.) Let me guess, he's never done this before.

DOWN LOW. *(To audience.)* I've never done this before. What am I doing?

> (**DOWN LOW** *snaps their fingers. Lights shift. Everyone unfreezes.*)

I've never done this before.

LOOKING. You don't say.

CASHIER. *(To* **COLLEGE STUDENT.**) How can I help you?!

> (**COLLEGE STUDENT** *snaps their fingers. Lights shift. Everyone freezes.*)

COLLEGE STUDENT. *(To audience.)* The cashier is on some sort of medication.

CASHIER. *(To audience.)* I am actually. All kinds of treatments. Diazepam. Valium, Temazepam, Zoloft, Lithium, HRT, ECT. You name it. I've had it. Combine that with coffee and I'm ready to go. At your service.

I find that I'm more myself, when I'm not myself. You know what I mean? It's like I live in an existential world, because frankly, who wants to live in the real world when all you have to do is lock yourself into a medicinal bubble. The world is nothing but a bottomless hellscape pushing every one of us to the brink of insanity. Take this corporation for example. We are told to provide service with a smile, so pardon me if my smile must be constructed with a bit of pharmaceuticals. My smile is a product of American capitalism so salute my teeth! Salute them! I love my job. I do. I love my job.

(**CASHIER** *snaps their fingers. Lights shift. Everyone unfreezes.*)

(To **COLLEGE STUDENT**.*)* HOW CAN I HELP YOU?

(A bell on the front door rings.)

(**FIRST GEN** *snaps their fingers. Light shift. Everyone freezes.*)

FIRST GEN. *(To audience.)* A person walks in. Could be bohemian. Could be unsheltered. I watch. They wear a dirty khaki jacket and a grungy overloaded bookbag. They look about twenty-five but could be younger. My eyes focus. They try to blend in, but I am on to them.

UNSHELTERED. *(To audience.)* I know they are staring. But hunger is more important than embarrassment.

FIRST GEN. *(To audience.)* They reach into the garbage pail and pull out a used cup. No one notices but me.

(**COLLEGE STUDENT** *snaps their fingers. Lights shift.*)

COLLEGE STUDENT. *(To audience.)* I do.

(**MANAGER** *snaps their fingers.*)

MANAGER. *(To audience.)* I do.

>   (**CASHIER** *snaps their fingers.*)

CASHIER. *(To audience.)* I do.

>   (**DOWN LOW** *snaps their fingers.*)

DOWN LOW. *(To audience.)* I do.

>   (**BARISTA** *snaps their fingers.*)

BARISTA. *(To audience.)* I do.

>   (**LOOKING** *snaps their fingers.*)

LOOKING. *(To audience.)* I do.

>   (**TABLE HOG** *snaps their fingers.*)

TABLE HOG. *(To audience.)* I do.

>   (*They all breathe and melt back into their last frozen pose.*)
>
>   (*Lights shift back to* **FIRST GEN**'s *perspective.*)

FIRST GEN. I watch. They work their way over to the counter, sprinkle nutmeg into the cup and grab the whole milk. None to be had. They reach for the half and half. Pour it until it reaches the lipstick stained rim. They quickly gulp down half, look over both shoulders, and refill once again, to the brim.

>   (**MANAGER** *awakens from the freeze upon hearing "well-dressed manager."*)

(To audience.) A well-dressed manager bumps into them and spills the half and half down the manager's shirt.

>   (**MANAGER** *walks past* **UNSHELTERED** *and they collide.*)
>
>   (*The cup is filled with white confetti. Confetti spills out.*)

(To audience.) They holler.

> (**FIRST GEN** *snaps their fingers. Lights shift. Everyone unfreezes.*)

MANAGER. You idiot!

UNSHELTERED. I'm sorry.

MANAGER. You shouldn't even be in here.

> (**UNSHELTERED** *sees all the patrons staring at them. They take in their disgust and internalize it. It's a moment.*)

> (**FIRST GEN** *snaps their fingers. Lights shift. Everyone freezes.*)

FIRST GEN. *(To audience.)* I feel for them. It wasn't long ago when Hurricane Sandy hit my family home and we hopped from air mattress, to cot, to sofa, to floor. My back still conditioned to the hardness of the ground while we waited for the insurance money to come through. This manager has never known what it's like to not know where you will sleep. To ration your food to survive until the next unemployment check. To take dozens of odd jobs you're overqualified for because it's all you can get when they hear your accent. This manager doesn't realize that we are all one step away from becoming this so-called idiot.

> *(Beat.)*

Bitch.

MANAGER. *(To audience.)* I was homeless from the age of two to eighteen. I worked for everything I have. I made it out. I got clean. I got a job... So can they.

FIRST GEN. *(To audience.)* Apologies commence.

> (**FIRST GEN** *snaps their fingers. Lights shift. Everyone unfreezes.*)

UNSHELTERED. I'm so sorry. Let me help...

MANAGER. Don't touch me, bum!

> *(Everyone looks away.)*

> *(**FIRST GEN** snaps their fingers. Lights shift. Everyone freezes.)*

FIRST GEN. *(To audience.)* I look away...not for their shame but mine. I judge myself for a split second, but then I taste the sweet flavor of my Pumpkin Spice latte, with the comfort in knowing that my lips are the only ones to have ever touched this cardboard cup. I forget everything I have just witnessed.

> *(**FIRST GEN** tries to snap out of the freeze, but their snap doesn't work.)*

> *(**TABLE HOG** is typing on a laptop and begins their inner dialogue while **FIRST GEN** keeps trying to make their snap work to unfreeze back into the real world.)*

TABLE HOG. *(To audience.)* Here I am hoping that my coffee addiction doesn't bleed my wallet too much before my new corporate drone job pays me my first paycheck. I've made the backwards leap from being a writer to ending up at a stupid office job working for my old high school principal who now works there because he was fired for kissing an underaged student. I guess that makes my foray back into corporate America all the more sleazy. But I tell my morals to deal because Mr. Shaev, my bankruptcy lawyer, doesn't give a shit about my morals. He sees dollar signs and who can blame him. That's why I took this job. It's not like I have buckets of –

> *(**FIRST GEN** snaps their fingers violently and almost falls onto **TABLE HOG**. The snap worked!)*

(Lights shift. Everyone unfreezes.)

FIRST GEN. Excuse me, do you know where the closest Apple store is?

*(**TABLE HOG** snaps their fingers. Lights shift. Everyone freezes.)*

TABLE HOG. *(To audience.)* Great! Now I've lost my train of thought. Don't they realize I am sitting here trying to write a brilliant piece of social commentary that is going to sell, sell, sell, and get me out of the hellhole that is now currently my life! APPARENTLY NOT! Now if this doesn't become a *New York Times* Bestseller, it will be this jerk's fault. They're lucky they didn't spill a drink on my laptop. Dr. Shaev is no joke. I'd have him sue the hell out this foreigner. Nearest Apple store? Do I look like a damn search engine? How about take two left turns up your ass!

*(**TABLE HOG** snaps their fingers. Lights shift. Everyone unfreezes.)*

*(To **FIRST GEN**.)* Soho. On Prince and Greene.

*(**FIRST GEN** walks past **DOWN LOW** just as **DOWN LOW** snaps their fingers.)*

(Lights shift. Everyone freezes.)

DOWN LOW. *(To audience.)* I imagine he is my boyfriend. That it's our first anniversary and we are planning to move in together. We put in an offer on a quaint brownstone in Cobble Hill, Brooklyn. I've always wanted to live in Brooklyn and with our combined incomes, it's possible! He wants to paint the living room blue, but I prefer warmer colors. We bicker in front of the paint chips at Home Depot for a while, but then, as any happy and emotionally stable couple does, we compromise. We settle on a blue and brown color palette. He tells me he would have never considered that color combination. I tell him that's why we are a team. He smiles and it is at that moment that I know that I love him.

LOOKING. *(To audience.)* I was never too much into the boyfriend experience. Starts out all exciting and passionate and then about a week or two in… Boredom. I sleep with someone else and leave. I don't really do intimacy. Why make yourself vulnerable to someone who is eventually going to use what you've shared with them against you to fulfill their own needs? People always talk about toxic relationships. Yeah, those are the intimate ones. "IT'S COMING FROM INSIDE THE HOUSE!" Hooking up and moving on is the healthiest thing you can do.

DOWN LOW. *(To audience.)* I want to marry him.

LOOKING. *(To audience.)* I have dinner plans at five.

DOWN LOW. *(To audience.)* I'm currently engaged to a wonderful girl with a great personality.

> (**DOWN LOW** *and* **LOOKING** *both snap at the same time. Lights shift. Everyone unfreezes.*)

MANAGER. I'm sorry but are you two going to order something?

| **DOWN LOW.** | **LOOKING.** |
| Yes. | No. |

MANAGER. You'll either have to order something or leave.

LOOKING. It's a public place.

MANAGER. It's a business and what you're doing is loitering.

LOOKING. Jeez.

> (**MANAGER** *snaps their fingers. Lights shift. Everyone freezes.*)

MANAGER. *(To audience.)* Nobody knows I hate my job.

    *(**COLLEGE STUDENT** snaps their fingers.)*

COLLEGE STUDENT. *(To audience.)* I do.

    *(**CASHIER** snaps their fingers.)*

CASHIER. *(To audience.)* I do.

    *(**TABLE HOG** snaps their fingers.)*

TABLE HOG. *(To audience.)* I do.

    *(**BARISTA** snaps their fingers.)*

BARISTA. *(To audience.)* I do.

    *(**UNSHELTERED** snaps their fingers.)*

UNSHELTERED. *(To audience.)* I do.

    *(**LOOKING** snaps their fingers.)*

LOOKING. *(To audience.)* I do.

    *(**FIRST GEN** snaps their fingers.)*

FIRST GEN. *(To audience.)* I do.

    *(**DOWN LOW** snaps their fingers.)*

DOWN LOW. *(To audience.)* I do.

    (They all breathe and melt back into their last frozen pose.)

    *(**DOWN LOW** snaps their fingers. Lights shift. Everyone unfreezes.)*

I'll get us some teas.

    *(**DOWN LOW** heads to the counter.)*

    (A bell on the front door rings.)

(**MANAGER** *snaps their fingers. Lights shift. Everyone freezes.*)

MANAGER. *(To audience.)* This must be my two o'clock. Even though it's two-fifteen, I'll deal. Nobody wants to work anymore. What are they calling it? The Great Resignation? But a job is a job. How could anyone walk away? I'd hire anyone with a pulse, at this point.

(**MANAGER** *sees* **UNSHELTERED** *still trying to clean up the mess.*)

(To audience.) Almost anyone.

(**MANAGER** *snaps their fingers. Lights shift. Everyone unfreezes.*)

Are you here for the two o'clock interview?

APPLICANT. I am.

MANAGER. You're late.

(**APPLICANT** *snaps their fingers. Lights shift. Everyone freezes.*)

APPLICANT. *(To audience.)* Red flag, number one. I'm interviewing them as much as they are interviewing me. Sure, I'm here because my parents told me to either go to college or pay rent. College is a crock. I'm not trying to be in debt for the rest of my life like my folks. The government can't even pass legitimate student debt relief because they are too busy wagging their finger screaming, "I had to pay so should you!" Shouldn't we want a better life for our children? You know what I'm not going to do? I'm not going to shame my kids for the benefits I receive, and you know why I'm not going to do that? Because I'll never receive any benefits from the government, so I won't be able to afford children. But you can bet everything that if I do happen to get pregnant, the government will make me have it anyway, so...

(**APPLICANT** *snaps their fingers. Lights shift. Everyone unfreezes.*)

Maybe I'm just extremely early. It's all about perspective.

MANAGER. Fill this out. I'll be back.

APPLICANT. Do you have a pen?

(**MANAGER** *snaps their fingers. Lights shift. Everyone freezes.*)

MANAGER. I hate her.

(**MANAGER** *snaps their fingers. Lights shift. Everyone unfreezes.*)

(**MANAGER** *hands her a pen and walks behind the counter.*)

(**APPLICANT** *tries to pass to a table, but* **UNSHELTERED** *is on their hands and knees cleaning up.*)

APPLICANT. Excuse me. I'm trying to pass. To fill this out. For a job.

UNSHELTERED. You should be so lucky.

(**APPLICANT** *snaps their fingers. Lights shift. Everyone freezes.*)

APPLICANT. *(To audience.)* Is this homeless person trying to come for me? Oh no.

(**APPLICANT** *snaps their fingers. Lights shift. Everyone unfreezes.*)

Move! Gross.

(*They step over* **UNSHELTERED** *and sits at a table.*)

(**COLLEGE STUDENT** *snaps their fingers. Lights shift. Everyone freezes.*)

COLLEGE STUDENT. *(To audience.)* I order my usual.

(**COLLEGE STUDENT** *snaps their fingers. Lights shift. Everyone unfreezes.*)

(To **CASHIER.***)* Soy chai, no foam, no water, grande.

CASHIER. Grande soy latte no foam no water chai?

COLLEGE STUDENT. Right. Soy chai, no foam, no water, grande.

CASHIER. *(Calling the order to* **BARISTA.***)* Grande soy latte no foam no water chai.

(**COLLEGE STUDENT** *snaps their fingers. Lights shift. Everyone freezes.*)

COLLEGE STUDENT. *(To audience.)* I hate them.

(**COLLEGE STUDENT** *snaps their fingers. Lights shift. Everyone unfreezes.*)

(To **CASHIER.***)* I'll take an espresso brownie as well.

CASHIER. One espresso brownie for the big fella.

(**COLLEGE STUDENT** *snaps their fingers. Lights shift. Everyone freezes.*)

COLLEGE STUDENT. *(To audience.)* It is at this point I decide they must die.

(**COLLEGE STUDENT** *snaps their fingers. Lights shift. Everyone unfreezes.*)

CASHIER. Name please.

COLLEGE STUDENT. Dakota.

CASHIER. I'm sorry?

COLLEGE STUDENT. Dakota.

CASHIER. North or South?

COLLEGE STUDENT. Funny.

CASHIER. One soy latte no foam no water chai and espresso brownie for Carolina.

COLLEGE STUDENT. Dakota.

CASHIER. One soy latte no foam no water chai and espresso brownie for Virginia.

COLLEGE STUDENT. Dakota.

CASHIER. Of course.

> *(During this interaction, **BARISTA** keeps writing and crossing out different names on different cups. **BARISTA** snaps their fingers. Lights shift. Everyone freezes.)*

BARISTA. *(To audience.)* I don't have a clue how to spell their name. This is the kind of stuff that your social media lives for. Don't act like you don't make fun of us baristas when we spell your name wrong, posting it to your Instagram stories…

"Look how dumb this barista is," and then you try to slyly get me in the photo as well. Yeah… I know you do it. But guess what? Jokes on you. We do it on purpose to drive more people to the hashtag you will inevitably include. It's also something to do to pass the time. Have you ever had to serve the public? It's akin to feeding animals at the zoo. They are all one step away from tearing your head off. I don't give a crap what your name is…

(To audience.) I just want the health benefits.

> *(**BARISTA** snaps their fingers. Lights shift. Everyone unfreezes.)*

APPLICANT. Excuse me. Does this job come with health benefits?

(Beat.)

BARISTA. No.

*(**BARISTA** walks away.)*

*(**COLLEGE STUDENT** hands **CASHIER** a gift card.)*

CASHIER. If you haven't registered this gift card online, it's really a good idea. If you lose it, you won't lose anything because it will be protected, and you can also get special gifts and prizes depending on how often you use the card. Would you listen to me! I sound like a commercial. HA! Your balance is on your receipt, have a great day, Alaska!

COLLEGE STUDENT. That's it. Dakota is my name. It's my name. It's who I am. And my name isn't here for your amusement. I am standing here ordering your capitalist drink. Your corporate antics have driven the mom-and-pop shops out of business. Now some silly-ass green siren is wooing us with fancy names for small, medium, and large. All I want is a chai and an outlet so I can write this damn paper on an epic poem that I will most definitely forget about the moment I hit send. So please...at the very least...you can get my damn name right.

BARISTA. Grande soy latte, no foam, no water chai for Wyoming!

*(**COLLEGE STUDENT** lets out a primal scream.)*

*(**COLLEGE STUDENT** snaps their fingers. Lights shift. Everyone freezes.)*

COLLEGE STUDENT. Does anyone care anymore?

(**CASHIER** *snaps their fingers.*)

CASHIER. I don't.

(**LOOKING** *snaps their fingers.*)

LOOKING. I don't.

(**FIRST GEN** *snaps their fingers.*)

FIRST GEN. I don't.

(**DOWN LOW** *snaps their fingers.*)

DOWN LOW. I don't.

(**TABLE HOG** *snaps their fingers.*)

TABLE HOG. I don't.

(**BARISTA** *snaps their fingers.*)

BARISTA. I don't.

(**APPLICANT** *snaps their fingers.*)

APPLICANT. I don't.

(**UNSHELTERED** *snaps their fingers.*)

UNSHELTERED. I do.

(**MANAGER** *somehow hears this. They grab the application out of* **APPLICANT***'s hands.*)

(**MANAGER** *snaps their fingers. They all breathe and melt back into their last frozen pose. Lights shift.*)

(*They hand the application to* **UNSHELTERED**.)

(**UNSHELTERED** *looks at the application with confusion.*)

MANAGER. Just a moment.

> (**MANAGER** *snatches the pen out of* **APPLICANT***'s hand.*)

APPLICANT. Hey!

> (**MANAGER** *hands the pen to* **UNSHELTERED**.)

UNSHELTERED. I don't understand.

MANAGER. Would you like to work here?

APPLICANT. WHAT?!

UNSHELTERED. I'm sorry?

APPLICANT. This is outrageous!

MANAGER. Would you like to work here?

APPLICANT. I'm trying to work here.

MANAGER. *(To* **APPLICANT**.*)* We're good, actually.

(To **UNSHELTERED**.*)* Would you like to work here?

UNSHELTERED. I don't have an address.

> (**MANAGER** *nods in a knowing way.*)

MANAGER. Let me see what I can do.

APPLICANT. Please. I need this job.

MANAGER. I think someone needs it more than you.

UNSHELTERED. What's the salary?

APPLICANT. Yeah. What's the salary?

MANAGER. $16.75 an hour.

> *(Beat.)*

APPLICANT.	**UNSHELTERED.**
I'll take it!	No, thanks.

MANAGER. What?

UNSHELTERED. I'm good. Thanks, though.

>(**UNSHELTERED** *walks out of the coffeehouse.*)

>(*Everyone in the coffeehouse snaps their finger except* **MANAGER** *and* **APPLICANT**.)

>(*Blackout.*)

End of Play

Kirdle & Miffins: Curiosity Saved the Cats

Book, Music & Lyrics by
Rona Siddiqui

KIRDLE & MIFFINS: CURIOSITY SAVED THE CATS premiered with Keen Company (Jonathan Silverstein, Artistic Director) as part of the Keen Teens Festival of New Work (Celestine Rae, Festival Artistic Director) at Theatre Row in New York City on May 19, 2023. The performance was directed by Tom Costello, with choreography by Laura K. Nicoll, music direction by Laurént G. Williams, sets by Indigo Shea, costumes by Brittani Beresford, lights by Alex DeNevers, and sound by Jordana Abrenica. The Production Stage Manager was Sloane Fischer. The cast was as follows:

KIRDLE	Kiesse Yengo-Passy
MIFFINS	Raizel Keisha Moscardon
RAISIN	Lily Daquigan
B-NUT	Angel Rodriguez
ZUCH	Isabella Lamacchia
GINGER	Charlotte Coffey
MALLO/BIG FOOT 1	Beatrice Rimel
SIMPLE SYRUP/BIG FOOT 2	Patience Lee Rodriguez
ELDERBERRY	Leonardo Kettells
FUKAMYS	Lily Giese

CHARACTERS

KIRDLE – A savvy street cat with a high intellect. Feels the burden of keeping Miffins and themselves alive out on the streets.

MIFFINS – Best buddy of Kirdle, Miffins has a big heart. They want to make Kirdle proud.

RAISIN – Dry sense of humor. Loner. Slight attitude about everything. Acts like they don't care. Demure. Likes to see other cats get into fights or fall from high places (as long as no one gets seriously hurt). Think Snape.

B-NUT – Jovial, high energy. but don't cross them cuz they'll f!@# you up. They'll go from laughing hysterically to attack mode on a dime. Think Tracy Morgan.

ZUCH – (Pronounced ZOO-k) Overthinks everything. Can never make a decision. But has opinions on everything too. Likes to talk. Wishy-washy, but wants to keep the peace. Can be anxious because so much is out of their control. Think Woody Allen.

GINGER – Fiery, natural born leader. They have no tolerance for BS. Get to the point! Quick-witted and confident. Think Bette Midler.

MALLO/BIG FOOT 1 – So fluffy and light on their feet, they're almost floating! They can sneak up on anyone at anytime and they do. They're a prankster. They love to observe the world around them. Equally happy to join on an adventure or curl up and take a nap.

SIMPLE SYRUP/BIG FOOT 2 – The baby of the group. Hyper to the point of annoyance, but full of loving energy. Not a bad thing to say about anyone ever. Even when someone takes a swipe at them. If they could play 24/7, they would. Napping is overrated. Loves Raisin for some inexplicable reason.

ELDERBERRY – The elder of the group. Wise and slow. Listens attentively, but never gets caught up in antics. Sleeps most of the time. Think Dumbledore.

FUKAMYS – (pronounced FOO-kuh-mees) Charismatic villain. Has only one concern. Making cheddar. They will do this at any cost and will employ any manipulation, trick, crime, etc. to keep the cheddar rolling in. They are a master of mind control.

AUTHOR'S NOTES

A note on pronouns: Any character can be any gender. Pronouns can be changed to suit the actor playing the role, or can remain they/them.

Scene One

Curio-city

[MUSIC NO. 01 – LIFE IN CURIO-CITY]

(Two cats, **KIRDLE** *and* **MIFFINS**, *roam the dark streets of Curio-city. It is a cool, artsy city landscape.)*

MIFFINS.
HEY KIRDLE?

KIRDLE.
YEAH MIFFINS?

MIFFINS.
WE BEEN UP ALL NIGHT ROAMING CURIO-CITY, MAN!
PROWLIN' AND SCOWLIN', DOGS HOWLIN', WOOF!
I CAN HARDLY STAND!

KIRDLE.
BUT I'M STILL STARVING.
ALL THE TRASH CAN LIDS ARE ON SO TIGHT

MIFFINS.
I'M SO HANGRY THINK I'LL START ANOTHER DUMPSTER FIGHT

KIRDLE.
NO NO!
LET'S GO TO DEADEND ALLEYWAY
JUST NEED ONE DROP OF MILK

MIFFINS.
OR SOME DUCK PÂTÉ

KIRDLE & MIFFINS.
>OKAY BESTIE, THEN WE'LL REST,
>SEE NIGHT IS ALMOST DONE
>WHEN WE'RE NICE AND FULL
>WE'LL CURL UP IN A PATCH OF SUN
>YEAH.

MIFFINS.
>HEY KIRDLE?

KIRDLE.
>YEAH MIFFINS?

MIFFINS.
>SOMETIMES THIS RAT RACE FEELS IMPOSSIBLE
>SO TIRED OF FIGHTING EV'RY OBSTACLE

KIRDLE.
>I HEAR YOU, MIFFS. WE NEED A LULL

MIFFINS.
>CURIO-CITY IS HARD

KIRDLE.
>BUT IT'S NEVER DULL.
>CURIO...

MIFFINS.
>KEEPS YOU ON YOUR TOES

KIRDLE.
>YEAH, IT'S NEVER DULL

MIFFINS.
>CURIO...

KIRDLE.
>MAKES YOU QUESTION WHAT YOU KNOW

MIFFINS.
>WHAT WILL YOU GO THROUGH TODAY?

KIRDLE.
>WHEN YOU'RE IN CURIO...

MIFFINS.
YUP, THAT'S RIGHT.

KIRDLE & MIFFINS.
WHEN YOU'RE IN CURIO
THAT'S LIFE IN CURIO-CITY

> *(They make it to Deadend Alleyway. There's no food to be found.)*

KIRDLE. Under that staircase?

MIFFINS. Nothing.

KIRDLE. Can you open up that trashbag?

MIFFINS. Nope. Too tight.

KIRDLE. Look! Is that a mouse?

MIFFINS. Yeah!

KIRDLE. Get it!

MIFFINS. No way! Look how cute it is! It's just trying to survive just like us.

KIRDLE. Well then my friend, I think we're out of luck.

MIFFINS. Hey, there's a car coming down the alley! Big Foots!

KIRDLE. They got Big Floofy last week!

MIFFINS. Not Big Floofy!!

KIRDLE. I searched for him for hours! No trace.

MIFFINS. Pour one out for Big Floof.

KIRDLE. Sh! Sh! They're coming!

MIFFINS. Assume the position! *(This means hide!)*

> *(They smoosh their bodies into weird shapes to hide behind or under or in random objects. A car pulls into the alley and* **TWO PEOPLE** *jump out, soldier style. They are scary in a* Home Alone *way.)*

BIG FOOT 1. Meer meer meer ran this way.

BIG FOOT 2. Meer block exit. Meer search.

BIG FOOT 1. Meeer mitty mitty mitty! Meeeeer mitty mitty mitty…

BIG FOOT 2. Meer see one!

[MUSIC NO. 01A – ALLEY CHASE]

> *(Chase scene! As **BIG FOOT 2** finds **KIRDLE** and lunges to grab them, **MIFFINS** leaps out of hiding to claw their ankle. This starts a wacky chase scene over, under, around, and through as many obstacles as can be put in an alleyway. **BIG FOOT 2** prevails in the end, finally ensnaring them in nets.)*

BIG FOOT 1. Meer these floofers to the mouse on McMougal.

BIG FOOT 2. Mopy mat.

> *(The **BIG FOOTS** put them in the van and drive away. In the darkness…)*

MIFFINS. Kirdle?

KIRDLE. Yeah Miffins?

MIFFINS. Where do you think we're going?

KIRDLE. I don't know, pal.

MIFFINS. We had a good run didn't we?

KIRDLE. Yeah pal. We did. There's no one on earth I'd rather have as my bestie in Curio-city than you. Thanks for always having my back.

MIFFINS. Yeah. Same. If I had to do it again, I wouldn't change a thing.

KIRDLE. Same… Except this part. This part I would probably change to eating duck pâté and then taking a nap.

MIFFINS. Yeah, that sounds nice.

KIRDLE. Yeah.

> *(Beat.)*

MIFFINS. Kirdle?

KIRDLE. Yeah Miffins?

MIFFINS. What are clouds and why can't I touch them? I've always wanted to know.

KIRDLE. I don't know. You know what I always wondered? Where that little grey squirrel hides her acorns. Or who that crazy robin was talking to up in that oak tree every morning.

MIFFINS. I tried to climb up there so many times to try to find out! …And also to eat it, if we're being honest.

KIRDLE. Well, I guess there are some things we'll never know.

MIFFINS. I'll never stop wanting to know.

KIRDLE. Me too, pal. Me too. I'll miss Curio-city

MIFFINS. Me too.

> *(Sound of van door opening. Lights up on **KIRDLE** and **MIFFINS** being tossed into an inviting living room space.)*

BIG FOOT 1. Meer meer meer new home!

BIG FOOT 2. Meer luck.

BIG FOOT 1. Meer meed it.

MIFFINS. Where are we?

KIRDLE. It smells like…

MIFFINS. …Duck pâté?

[MUSIC NO. 02 – COMPLACEN-CITY]

(*Slowly* **CATS** *poke out from hiding places and slowly approach* **KIRDLE** *and* **MIFFINS**. *Then suddenly...*)

RAISIN.
>COMPLACEN-CITY!

GINGER.
>OH-OO-WHOA!

ZUCH.
>WELCOME TO COMPLACEN-CITY!

B-NUT.
>COMPLACEN-CITY!

SIMPLE SYRUP.
>OH-OO-WHOA!

MALLO.
>YOU ARE IN COMPLACEN-CITY
>THE PLACE WHERE YOU CAN VEG OUT ALL DAY

GINGER.
>WHERE YOU FILL YOUR BELLY AT THE CAT BUFFET

SIMPLE SYRUP.
>WHERE YOU CAN PLAY ALL DAY

ELDERBERRY.
>OR DREAM AWAY

RAISIN.
>IN A PATCH OF SUN

ALL.
>COMPLACEN-CITY OH-OO-WHOA!
>YOU ARE IN COMPLACEN-CITY
>COMPLACEN-CITY OH!

MALLO.
>AND WATCH ALL YOUR CARES MELT AWAY

B-NUT. (*Rapping.*)
>COMPLACEN-CITY IS THE PLACE TO BE, BABY

KIRDLE & MIFFINS: CURIOSITY SAVED THE CATS   37

YOU WANNA TOUR? COME AND FOLLOW ME, BABY!
YOU SEE THOSE BOWLS? YUP. THAT'S WHERE WE SUP.
AND LOOK UP, IF YOU WILL AND SEE A SILL FOR YOU TO
    PERCH UPON,
OR LURK UPON
OR TWERK UPON!
HEY, I DON'T JUDGE, BABY, YOU CAN GO BERSERK UPON!
AND WE GOT COUCHES AND TOY MOUSES JUST FEAST
    YOUR EYES!
EV'RY DAY IS TUNA SALAD! AND CLEAR BLUE SKIES.
YOU'LL LIVE YOUR DAYS WITHOUT A STARTLE OR A
    SURPRISE

(Having snuck up behind **KIRDLE** *and* **MIFFINS** *and now deftly leaping out:)*

MALLO.
BOO!

B-NUT. *(Shrug.)*
JUST KIDDING!

ALL (EXCEPT SIMPLE SYRUP).	**SIMPLE SYRUP.**
COMPLACEN-CITY OH-OO-WHOA!	YEAH YEAH
WELCOME TO COMPLACEN-CITY	YEAH
COMPLACEN-CITY OH-OO-WHOA!	YEAH YEAH

GINGER, RAISIN
& ELDERBERRY

AND WATCH YOUR CARES MELT AWAY	YEAH

MALLO, ZUCH & B-NUT
    AND WATCH YOUR CARES
        MELT AWAY

GINGER, RAISIN & ELDERBERRY

COMPLACEN-CITY	YEAH

ALL (EXCEPT SIMPLE SYRUP).

OH-OO-WHOA!	YEAH
YOU ARE IN COMPLACEN-CITY	YEAH

ALL.

>COMPLACEN-CITY OH-OO-WOAH!
>AND WATCH YOUR CARES MELT AWAY

KIRDLE. Um...thank you?

MIFFINS. Um yeah...so...who are you?

GINGER. Oh goshy forgive their manners! I'm Ginger. I keep these cats in line. Let's go dummies. State your names and make our new friends feel at home.

SIMPLE SYRUP. *(Waving vigorously.)* Hiiii!!! Hello!!! I'm Simple Syrup. I can't wait to play with you allll day!!! Okay bye!

B-NUT. B-Nut's the name. I'm down for your antics if you've got any, but you mess with me and I will not take no –

ZUCH. Oh no oh no oh no!! B-Nut, no one is messing with you. Oh dear. So touchy, so sensitive. I'm Zuch. Ya know I was just saying to Ginger the other day how my tum tum has been bothering me, and you know what she said? Too much duck pâté! Can you believe that? So, I switched over to the diced salmon for the last few days and I feel magnificent. Never better!

MALLO. Mmm. Salmon.

GINGER. Mallo. Want to introduce yourself?

MALLO. Mallo! Just ya know. Doing my thing. Which is anything really. I just go with the flow.

>*(They reach a paw out to shake with **MIFFINS**. **MIFFINS** shakes **MALLO**'s paw, but one of those noise buzzers is on it, and it emits a loud sound. **MIFFINS** jumps and near hits the ceiling!)*

Hehehe. Gotcha!

GINGER. Raisin?

RAISIN. Hm?

GINGER. Wanna introduce yourself?

RAISIN. I think you just did, no?

ZUCH. Oh my goodness so rude, Raisin!

RAISIN. Mind your own business, Zuch

B-NUT. Don't you *mess* with Zuch!

RAISIN. Simmer down "*Pea*nut!"

B-NUT. You know it's B-Nut! You know it's not Peanut! I'ma f–

> (**ELDERBERRY** *rises slowly during this tirade and places a gentle paw on* **B-NUT***'s shoulder, quieting them.*)

ELDERBERRY. And I am Elderberry. I have been here the longest. I have seen just about everything there is to see. And I am happy to welcome you here to Complacen-City.

KIRDLE. I'm Kirdle and this is Miffins.

MIFFINS. Hello!

KIRDLE. Well nice meeting everyone. We'll just be on our way now.

MIFFINS. Thanks for the song. Good beat. Everyone on key. Really nice. Bye!

> (**KIRDLE** *and* **MIFFINS** *start to look for a way back out.*)

GINGER. Oh. Kirdle… Miffins… Did you *want* to go back to Curio-city?

MIFFINS. Well that's our home, so…yeah…but maybe we could get a little of that duck pâté for the road?

KIRDLE. Oh yes, a kitty bag would be great and then we'll see ourselves out. Thank you so much.

ZUCH. I don't think they understand. Do they understand?

SIMPLE SYRUP. You're my new best friends!

RAISIN. They're trying to tell you. You've been caught by Big Foots.

GINGER. That was scary we know, but Big Foots are not so bad. They bring us tons of food and water everyday. Curio-city is just a bunch of questions: Where will I sleep? What will I eat? Who can I trust? How do I survive? But Complacen-City has all the answers! Anywhere, all the food, everyone, and easily!

B-NUT. It's the shiz-nuts. We got you, little sibs!

MALLO. Take a load off those paws and relax!

GINGER. Cats! You know what time it is??

ALL BUT KIRDLE & MIFFINS. GRUB TIME!

> (*All the* **CATS** *run to the bowls. They are empty! The* **CATS** *are baffled.*)

ZUCH. What in the...

SIMPLE SYRUP. But I'm hungry! Why didn't the Big Foots fill the bowls?

GINGER. I'm sure there's a good reason! This is Complacen-City! We don't need to ask questions!

ELDERBERRY. Let's not panic. Mind over bellies. We'll be just fine.

RAISIN. Well, might as well just go to sleep then. I bid you all adieu. If you need me, too bad. You won't know where to find me. I'm sure you will all make it through the night without knowledge of my place of repose.

SIMPLE SYRUP. Oh you mean in the nook between the couch and the ottomon?

RAISIN. (*...Glare.*) ...Yes that is indeed where I'll be.

SIMPLE SYRUP. Okay I'll be under the couch right next to you, Raisin! Just like every night. Love you, Raisin.

RAISIN. *(...Sigh.)* ...Very well, Simple Syrup.

B-NUT. I'm on prowl duty. I got the perimeter on *lock*! I'll wake y'all up if the grub comes.

ZUCH. Hey where'd Mallo go?

> *(**MALLO** is standing right behind **ZUCH**.)*

MALLO. Good night, Zuch!

ZUCH. *(Startled.)* Ah!! Everyday, I tell you. Everyday, ya ball of fluff! Goodnight, Mallo.

GINGER. Goodnight everybody. Catnip dreams!

> *(**KIRDLE** and **MIFFINS** curl up next to each other.)*

MIFFINS. Hey Kirdle?

KIRDLE. Yeah Miffins?

MIFFINS. I think we're gonna like it here.

KIRDLE. No more struggle, buddy.

MIFFINS. Hey Kirdle?

KIRDLE. Yeah Miffins?

MIFFINS. I'd be lost without you. I'm glad we're still together.

KIRDLE. Aw Miffs, you'd be fine without me! You're one of the most curious cats I know!

MIFFINS. Not like you though. You always come up with the best plans. You've kept us alive.

KIRDLE. We've kept each other alive.

> *(**MIFFINS** snuggles up to **KIRDLE**. They fall asleep.)*

[MUSIC NO. 02A – THE RISE OF FUKAMYS]

(Lights out. In the darkness we hear the voice of **FUKAMYS** *[Pronounced FOO-kuh-mees.])*

FUKAMYS. Kitties... Oh kitties...wondering where your vittles went, you insufferable felines? Did one of you hoard it all? Did the Big Foots abandon you? Ah but you're too...*complacent* to ask any questions aren't you. You don't care where your next meal comes from. Even if it's in...BASEMENT!

(They hum a hypnotic tune, then laugh.)

Ahahahaha. AAAAHahahahaha!!!!

(In the darkness we see a pair of mouse ears rise. They cast an ominous shadow on the wall.)

(Blackout.)

Scene Two

The next day in Complacen-city

GINGER. *(Cat stretches.)* Ahhhh. Another great day in Complacen-city. Morning everyone. Food status?

B-NUT. Negative. Starting to feel a little woozy, to be honest.

GINGER. B-Nut, take a nap. You'll feel better. I'm sure the Big Foots will arrive soon. I'm gonna hit the litter first if nobody minds.

ELDERBERRY. I beat you to it, dear Ginger. This elder bladder seldom holds all night hehe.

ZUCH. Well I'll wait my turn in line. No problem for me, and no accidents since the switch to salmon. I'm telling you I feel light as a feather. Almost as light as Mallo! Isn't that right, Mallo... Mallo? ...Oh haha you're probably right behind me aren't you haha! *(Turns around. No Mallo.)* Raisin, where's Mallo?

RAISIN. And how the fish should I know?

ZUCH. And why isn't Simple Syrup bouncing all over your head right now like usual?

RAISIN. Again you ask a question I have neither the knowledge nor care to answer.

B-NUT. Come to think of it, I haven't seen either one this morning. Maybe the new cats saw them?

MIFFINS. I was out cold!

KIRDLE. Same. I've never slept so hard in my whole life.

RAISIN. I'm sure they'll turn up. Now excuse me while I go nap.

B-NUT. You just woke up!

RAISIN. Wow. What commanding powers of observation, *pea*-nut.

B-NUT. It's B-Nut, man, *come* on!

MIFFINS. Do you think we should form a search party to look for Mallo and Simple Syrup?

GINGER. Nah. Things usually find a way of working themselves out here...

KIRDLE. Hm. The way I see it, we have two major problems. One: No food. Two: Missing cats. Are they related? Has either event happened before?

ZUCH. Yup.

MIFFINS. What? Why didn't anyone say that?

GINGER. It's not our place to ask questions. Cats can come and go. And food? Eventually some will turn up.

KIRDLE. And no one is wondering why?

B-NUT. I wonder why, but also, I like to be an easygoing cat. No need to ruffle any fur.

MIFFINS. So this is Complacen-city huh? You just let life happen to you?

B-NUT. ...Yes?

KIRDLE. I don't buy it. Someone has to do something to solve this mystery or cats may keep disappearing and we all may starve! Let's be on the hunt for clues. Sniff out traces of Mallo and Simple Syrup's fur, look for any holes or cracks you haven't noticed before. Where do the Big Foots keep the food? Can we access it?

GINGER. Wow, how do you know to do all that?

KIRDLE. Out in Curio-city, the best way to solve a mystery is to keep your eyes peeled, and question everyone. Somebody has to have seen something,

MIFFINS. Kirdle, maybe you could interview everyone over there.

RAISIN. Oh look, a patch of sun. I'll go…"investigate."

(**RAISIN** *saunters off, disinterested.*)

GINGER. *(To* **KIRDLE.***)* Well, good luck with your investigation.

(Lights out.)

[MUSIC NO. 2B – INTERVIEW SEQUENCE]

(Lights back up on an interrogation type area where **KIRDLE** *is pacing back and forth while the interrogated* **CATS** *rotate rapidly into and out of a chair at a table, getting questioned.)*

KIRDLE. *(To* **ZUCH.***)* And so whereabouts were you at 11:45 last night, Zuch?

ZUCH. Oh dear, I already told you! I had just a little bit of a furball in my throat, so I walked around the corner to cough it up in private! I didn't want to disturb anyone. You know how annoying it is getting woken up by a cough, right?

KIRDLE. *(To* **B-NUT.***)* B-Nut, how many times has Mallo disappeared and then reappeared?

B-NUT. Hundreds probably! And every time it gets my heart *pounding*.

KIRDLE. *(To* **MIFFINS.***)* Did you see anything out of the ordinary last night.

MIFFINS. Everything is out of the ordinary! It's our first day here!

KIRDLE. Fair fair.

(Back to **ZUCH.***)* And after you coughed up that furball, what did you do?

ZUCH. I went right back to sleep. I've got to get my twelve hours you know. Otherwise I'm just an anxious mess! I know, hard to believe!

KIRDLE. *(Back to* **B-NUT.***)* So nothing was out of place on your perimeter sweep, B-Nut?

B-NUT. Well there was one doorknob that seemed a bit askew if you will, but I, B-Nut, know not how to turn a doorknob so... I left it alone. Figured it was no big deal.

KIRDLE. *(To* **GINGER.***)* Ginger, which cats know how to turn a doorknob?

GINGER. Hm... None that I know of, but if anyone could, it would probably be Mallo. They've got the highest hops and the quickest reflexes...

KIRDLE. Elderberry, did you see anything out of the ordinary last night?

ELDERBERRY. No but I did have a strange dream about... cheese.

KIRDLE. *(Ah the rantings of an old person.)* Okay...

ELDERBERRY. They were in a dark room making cheese...

KIRDLE. Right...

ELDERBERRY. And I could smell the cheese too... Although come to think of it, it could have been gas...

KIRDLE. Mmhmm. Maybe you should go take a nap, Elderberry.

ELDERBERRY. Don't mind if I do.

KIRDLE. *(Has their back turned. Thinks they're about to talk to* **RAISIN.***)* And what about you, Raisin. You've been awfully quiet about this whole thing.

FUKAMYS. *(In disguise as a cat.)* Well I did see something.

KIRDLE. *(Whips around excitedly. Sees this new "cat.")* Oh! Who are you? I don't think we met yesterday...

FUKAMYS. Ah yes, I was on a little vacation. Yes, I'm... Mumyow. *(Pronounced Muh-MYOW.)*

KIRDLE. ...Mumyow?

FUKAMYS. Mumyow. Yes Mumyow.

KIRDLE. So what did you see... Mumyow?

FUKAMYS. Well I got in kind of late so I curled up behind the couch, see? And in the darkness, I saw a cat tiptoe toward the buffet.

KIRDLE. Was there food?

FUKAMYS. Well how should I know! I'm just a complacent cat who doesn't ask questions. But maybe...

KIRDLE. Yes...?

FUKAMYS. Maybe there *was* food...

KIRDLE. But there was no food this morning...

FUKAMYS. No. No there wasn't...

KIRDLE. And did you see who it was? Who went to the buffet? Was it Mallo? Simple Syrup?

FUKAMYS. Oh I shouldn't say. Maybe there's a good reason.

KIRDLE. Tell me!

FUKAMYS. Well you twisted my whiskers. Who's the one cat who didn't seem that hungry this morning? Who seems the least affected? It was... / Raisin!!!!

KIRDLE. / Raisin!

> *(Thunder and lightning! The lights flicker off.* **FUKAMYS** *exits. We hear a hypnotic tune, then the lights come back on.)*

(Has back to the interview chair.) Now where did you say you came from, Mumyow?

> *(When* **KIRDLE** *spins back around to address "Mumyow" they are gone.)*

Hmmm.

MIFFINS. Is it my turn again?

KIRDLE. No Miffins. It's time to go talk to Raisin.

MIFFINS. Where is Raisin?

KIRDLE. In the sun, no doubt. Let's go!

> *(On the hunt throughout the house.)*

(Calling out.) Raisin?

MIFFINS. Raiiiisin! Where are you?

> *(The other remaining **CATS** join in the search for **RAISIN**.)*

ALL. *(Ad-lib.)* Raisin? Where are you?

GINGER. They're gone!

KIRDLE. On the run!

ZUCH. You think Raisin ate all the food? I don't believe it. I just don't believe it!

GINGER. And that still doesn't explain where Mallo and Simple Syrup are.

KIRDLE. Well Mumyow said they saw / Raisin last night...

B-NUT. / Who?

GINGER. Who's Mumyow?

KIRDLE. You don't know Mumyow?

ELDERBERRY. In my many years here I have never come across a... Mumyow.

KIRDLE. Then who was that cat???

MIFFINS. And where is Raisin???

> *(Thunder and lightning.)*

GINGER. This is getting creepy.

KIRDLE. B-Nut, you mentioned a doorknob that was askew. Where is it? Is it still out of alignment?

B-NUT. Nah. It's back to normal again. Maybe I just imagined it.

ELDERBERRY. Did I mention I had a dream about cheese?

KIRDLE. Yes you did, Elderberry… Very…helpful.

GINGER. Okay. Slow perimeter. B-Nut. You take lead.

KIRDLE. I'll bring up the rear.

MIFFINS. I'll be in the middle if that's okay…

ZUCH. You and me both. My old ticker ain't what it used to be. I can't take all this excitement!

> *(The lights suddenly go out. Lightning strikes. Thunder shakes the house.)*

ELDERBERRY. Nothing to fear. Just a storm. Just a storm.

> *(The **CATS** continue to walk slowly in a blob around the house, inspecting as they go. During the next few lines, **KIRDLE** stealthily exits.)*

ZUCH. Right right right. Nothing to fear. Just the lights going out and a bunch of cats missing.

B-NUT. Everyone still behind me? Sound off!

GINGER. Yup.

ELDERBERRY. Right here.

MIFFINS. Present and accounted for.

ZUCH. I'm still here.

> *(…)*
>
> *(…)*

MIFFINS. Kirdle? …Kirdle you still got rear??

> *(They turn around. **KIRDLE** is gone.)*

ALL. KIRDLE!!!!

    (Lights out.)

Scene Three

Basement – A Cheddar factory

(**SIMPLE SYRUP, MALLO, RAISIN,** *and* **KIRDLE** *are in a dank, windowless basement. There is a cheddar-making machine. One cat is doing a churning motion, one cat is draining and sifting through a colander, one cat is forming curds into a circular pan and pressing it, and one cat is packaging. This can all be pantomimed or be on an elaborate "machine" set piece.)*

FUKAMYS. Ah kitties. You are doing such a great job already! You've only been making cheddar for a day and you're experts at it! Tell me, do you love your new job?

SIMPLE SYRUP, MALLO, RAISIN & KIRDLE. *(Like zombies.)* Yes Fukamys.

FUKAMYS. Good kitties. Do you know why you're making cheddar?

SIMPLE SYRUP, MALLO, RAISIN & KIRDLE. No Fukamys.

FUKAMYS. Because I was but a poor mouse. Bullied, picked on, chased, and tormented. By whom, you might ask?

(They don't ask.)

By cats of course. They saw me as a little toy to bat around, at best! A meal at worst. But I survived. And I swore that one day, I would...*allow* cats the opportunity to make things right, and become the most powerful mouse in the world! So I found this basement beneath this "wonderful" cat sanctuary, and decided to take back what is mine... My dignity. So you see, kitties, thanks to the Big Foots under my command, you are my forever "volunteers" now, and I will benefit from the toils of your labor until you can toil no longer. Do you love your new overlord, I mean, employer, Fukamys?

SIMPLE SYRUP, MALLO, RAISIN & KIRDLE. We love you, Fukamys.

FUKAMYS. Yes, my little Complacents. Tell me Simple Syrup. What's your favorite toy?

SIMPLE SYRUP. I live to work and please you, Fukamys.

FUKAMYS. And Mallo, you feel like pulling any pranks today?

MALLO. I feel like making you more cheddar, Fukamys.

FUKAMYS. And what about you, Raisin? Missing your precious sunshine?

RAISIN. You are my sunshine now, Fukamys.

FUKAMYS. That's right, Raisin. That's right. And Kirdle. Tough street cat, Kirdle. Bet you're missing your little friend Miffins about now, aren't you?

KIRDLE. *(...)*

FUKAMYS. Oh Kirrrrdle... Answer the QUESTION! Are you missing your little friend Miffins?

KIRDLE. You are my only friend, Fukamys.

FUKAMYS. That's right, Kirdle. Now work faster!! All of you!! No sleeping on the job! More cheddar! More cheddar!! Ahahahahaha!!!!

SIMPLE SYRUP, MALLO, RAISIN & KIRDLE. More cheddar. More cheddar.

(Lights out.)

(Back to Complacen-City.)

MIFFINS. The only thing we have to go on is a bent doorknob. *(Sigh.)* I'm at a loss. Gah! Kirdle would know what to do! Anyone have any ideas?

(They all shrug at each other and shake their heads disappointedly.)

B-Nut. Will you take us to the doorknob? Maybe we can think of a way to open the door.

B-NUT. Open a door?? Im*poss*ible! But, I'll take you over there.

ELDERBERRY. B-Nut, nothing is impossible. It is the limitations of our own minds that make us believe it is impossible. But if we expand the limitations of our minds...we can see the problem in a new way.

ZUCH. Deep Elderberry. I want to expand my mind, but we didn't even eat dinner! Can I expand my tum first with some salmon pâté?

ELDERBERRY. This is the very time to expand your mind! Our greatest change comes in moments of discomfort.

ZUCH. I'll take your word for it, old pal.

MIFFINS. So if anything is possible, then I'm going to say right now. We will open that door. I know if Kirdle was here they'd already have it figured out. So all I need to do is imagine my brain is as big as Kirdle's.

*(**MIFFINS** closes their eyes and imagines.)*

To the door!

(They walk to the door to the basement. The doorknob is the L-shaped kind.)

B-NUT. Now I've seen Big Foots do this a million times. You just grab it and press.

GINGER. Right. Can you reach it?

B-NUT. No.

GINGER. *(To **ZUCH**.)* Can you?

ZUCH. *(Tries. Barely gets a paw on it.)* No.

MIFFINS. What can we stand on?

B-NUT. Each other. Pile on!

> *(They try to pyramid up to the doorknob, but fall all over each other.)*

GINGER. Nope.

ZUCH. There's that ball over there...

> *(**ZUCH** points to a big beach ball across the room.)*

GINGER. No way. We're too heavy and could never balance on that.

MIFFINS. Okay, but maybe we can use it another way...

ZUCH. What. Throw the ball at the doorknob?

B-NUT. That's crazy. Maybe if I run back and forth I can work up my speed and jump mad high!

> *(He starts running around everyone like a crazy cat.)*

GINGER. Cut it out, B-Nut! I can't concentrate!

MIFFINS. Wait. I've got it. I met an escaped cat from the circus once in Curio-city. They used to launch him into the air with a catapult!

B-NUT. A c*at*apult?

ZUCH. You can't be serious.

MIFFINS. Yes! Okay. Is there a long flat piece of wood somewhere?

GINGER. Yes! Elderberry's ramp to the couch!

MIFFINS. B-Nut, can you go drag that over here?

B-NUT. Yes I can!

MIFFINS. Great! Okay, who's the heaviest and who's the lightest?

ZUCH. I'm not following what we're doing here.

MIFFINS. We're going to launch one of us high into the air over the top off the doorknob, so that on the way down, we can grab it and pull it open!

GINGER. Genius!

B-NUT. I've got the most mass.

ELDERBERRY. And I'm clearly the lightest of the bunch.

GINGER. No way, Elderberry. No stunts for you!

B-NUT. Yeah my dude. We need you to keep it four on the floor.

ELDERBERRY. My cats. If this is the last thing I can do to save our friends and solve this mystery, I will gladly give my last life.

ZUCH. *(Tearing up.)* No. No!

ELDERBERRY. Zucchini. Let me do this. It's the best plan we've got.

> (**ZUCH** *nods and looks away.* **B-NUT** *has brought the plank over and positioned it over the ball.*)

MIFFINS. Elderberry, you sit on the far side, but face the door. B-Nut, get a running start, pounce on the other side, and that should send Elderberry flying up and over. Keep your eye on the knob. Grab it. Pull down and out.

ELDERBERRY. I understand the assignment. Let's go.

GINGER. Good luck!

> (**ELDERBERRY** *takes their position.* **B-NUT** *runs at the plank and jumps down on it.* **ELDERBERRY** *goes flying up. On the way down, they grab the doorknob, pull and open it. The door flies open!* **ELDERBERRY** *lands with a thud.*)

ZUCH. Oh my goodness are you okay?! Talk to us!!

(**ELDERBERRY** *winces in pain.*)

I'll...be...fine. Go. Save our friends.

GINGER. We're not going to leave you here alone!

ELDERBERRY. Zucchini Branch McKnuckles. Ginger Bread Toadstool, Butternut Squash McGee, and Miffins...

MIFFINS. Yeah it's just Miffins...

ELDERBERRY. Miffins. You must do this. There is no time to lose... Do you smell that? ...Cheese... Am I dreaming?

B-NUT. It *does* smell like cheese!

(**ELDERBERRY** *closes their eyes.*)

ZUCH. Elderberry!!

ELDERBERRY. (*Weakly with eyes closed.*) Go...

MIFFINS. You are a hero, Elderberry. Now let's go rescue some cats!

(*They tiptoe down the stairs and hide behind something as they witness* **FUKAMYS** *lounging around while* **SIMPLE SYRUP**, **MALLO**, **RAISIN**, *and* **KIRDLE** *continue to make cheddar.*)

FUKAMYS. It's funny, you never asked me how I lured you down to my cheddar factory. Not that it matters. There's nothing you can do about it now. But I'm such a clever mouse and I like to tell everyone how clever I am. Do you want to know?

SIMPLE SYRUP, MALLO, RAISIN & KIRDLE. Yes, Fukamys.

FUKAMYS. I've spent years giving you everything you could possibly want so that you'd lose your curiosity. Then every so often, when the food stops for a couple days, and a cat or two go missing, no one asks any questions.

KIRDLE & MIFFINS: CURIOSITY SAVED THE CATS

Brilliant, I know. So my minions, the Big Foots, stop feeding you. Big Foots love cheddar too you know. They can't resist it. That's how I keep them under my control. At night, they leave a path of cheddar right to the basement door. They crack the door ever so slightly. Someone's rumbling tum tum inevitably draws them toward the bait and then! *(Thunder and lightning.)* New kitty volunteers to make me cheddar. So simple!

And once you're down here, I lay my little Song of Truhth *(Sounds like "truck" but ending with "th".)* on you.

*(**ZUCH** bravely comes out from hiding.)*

ZUCH. You mean *truth*?

*(**B-NUT**, **GINGER**, and **ZUCH** trepidatiously also come out of hiding.)*

FUKAMYS. Ah welcome newcomers! Right on schedule. You're just in time for my Song of Truhth. No Zuch. The *truhth* is better than the *truth* because it's more... malliable. More flexible if you will.

ZUCH. You mean a lie?

FUKAMYS. NO YOU IDIOT! *(Now demurely.)* Truhth is an art. It tells the Complacents, *you* Complacents, everything you want to hear so I can go about my "business" in peace! It's hypnotic really. Listen...

[MUSIC NO. 03 – SONG OF TRUHTH]

KITTY CATS ARE SPECIAL
THEY HAVE SO MUCH PROWESS
LOOK HOW CLEVER MEOW MEOW MEOW
MUCH MORE SO THAN A MOWUS
CHEDDAR MAKES THE WORLD GO ROUND
I GIVE *MINE* ALL AWAY
TO NEEDY LITTLE CATCOMPOOPS

FUKAMYS.
>I MEAN... THE SICK AND THE STRAY
>YES, I'M A HERO I'M A GOD
>THE FINEST GOOD SAMARITAN
>OUR FLOWING CHEDDAR HEALS THE WORLD
>OF THAT, I AM CER-I-TAN
>YOU HAVE ALL THE ANSWERS NOW
>THERE'S NOTHING LEFT TO KNOW
>THAT'S THE TRUHTH. I CROSS MY HEART
>NOW MAKE THAT CHEDDAR FLOW
>CATS BE NIMBLE, CATS BE QUICK
>GIVE THE OLD HEAVE HO!
>FUKAMYS NOW REIGNS SUPREME
>SO MAKE THAT CHEDDAR FLOW!

>*(Hypnotized by the song,* **B-NUT**, **GINGER**, *and* **ZUCH** *join the factory line.)*

B-NUT, GINGER & ZUCH.
>MAKE THAT CHEDDAR FLOW

FUKAMYS.
>MAKE THAT CHEDDAR FLOW!

>Here you have nothing to think about. Nothing to fear. We work to feel closer to Fukamys.

ALL CATS. We feel closer to Fukamys

FUKAMYS. We love Fukamys

ALL CATS. We love Fukamys

FUKAMYS. We will sacrifice our lives for the cheddar.

ALL CATS.	**MIFFINS.**
We will –	NO!!!!!!!!!!!

>*(**MIFFINS** comes swinging from a chandelier.)*

FUKAMYS.	**MIFFINS.**
What the!	CURIOSITY FOREVER!!!!

(**MIFFINS** *lands on top of the cheddar machine, destroying it.*)

FUKAMYS. No. Nonononono! Reassemble the machine! NOW!

(**ELDERBERRY** *hobbles in and with a commanding voice calls out each name to snap them out of the trance.*)

ELDERBERRY. Simple Syrup, Mallo, Raisin, Kirdle, Ginger, B-Nut, Zuch!

KIRDLE. Miffins??

MIFFINS. Kirdle!!

(*They embrace.*)

ALL CATS. Elderberry!

(**ELDERBERRY** *has collapsed. They rush to their side.*)

GINGER. Are they alive?

ZUCH. Barely.

FUKAMYS. Everyone back to work! Remember?

(*A capella.*)
YOU HAVE ALL THE ANSWERS NOW
THERE'S NOTHING LEFT TO KNOW

(*The* **CATS** *are no longer susceptible to Fukamys's hypnotic song.*)

B-NUT. Actually, there's a lot left to know! And now we want answers.

FUKAMYS. Right yes of course... But first...you're gonna have to catch me!

(**FUKAMYS** *scurries off running. He tries the basement stairs but is blocked. He tries all sorts of ways out, but the* **CATS** *form a strong defensive perimeter and* **FUKAMYS** *has nowhere to turn.* **B-NUT** *takes* **FUKAMYS** *by the arm.)*

KIRDLE. What happened to the other cats that disappeared before us?

FUKAMYS. Let's just say...they worked so hard they burned through all nine of their lives pretty quickly. That's why I had to keep replenishing the work force.

ZUCH. You evil bastard!

FUKAMYS. You call it evil, I call it industrious! That's the truhth.

MIFFINS. And where is the cheddar really going? The *TRUTH*!

FUKAMYS. In my pocket of course! So I could live the good life. A shopping spree in New Hamsterdam? Dinner in Papua New Guinea Pig? Mouscar De La Renta jewelry? I deserve it. I deserve it all!

SIMPLE SYRUP. *(Confused and still coming around.)* Raisin? Where are we?

RAISIN. Stay behind me, Simple Syrup.

*(***RAISIN** *approaches* **FUKAMYS** *slowly.)*

I'm going to say this once so listen carefully. You. Can. NEVER smother our curiosity. You may have lulled us momentarily, but now we're awake. We're paying attention. And we will never let anyone stop us from asking questions again.

KIRDLE. Especially when we know something nefarious is going down.

SIMPLE SYRUP. Yeah! Nefarious! ...What's nefarious?

[MUSIC NO. 04 – THAT'S HOW CURIOSITY SAVED THE CATS]

KIRDLE & MIFFINS.
CURIOSITY'S WHAT MAKES US GREAT

MALLO & GINGER.
WE KEEP IT REAL AND SEEK THE FACTS

ZUCH & SIMPLE SYRUP.
THINK BEFORE YOU TAKE THE BAIT

ALL.
AND THAT'S HOW CURIOSITY SAVED THE CATS

RAISIN & B-NUT.
CURIOSITY'S WHAT MAKES US STRONG

ELDERBERRY & MALLO.
SHINE A LIGHT INTO THE CRACKS

KIRDLE & MIFFINS.
ASK BEFORE YOU GO ALONG

ALL.
AND THAT'S HOW CURIOSITY SAVED THE CATS
THAT'S HOW CURIOSITY SAVED THE CATS
WE KEEP IT REAL AND WE SEEK THE FACTS
WE SHINE A LIGHT INTO THE CRACKS
AND THAT'S HOW CURIOSITY SAVED THE

*(The **CATS** kick **FUKAMYS** off the stage.)*

CATS!!!!!!

(Blackout.)

End of Show

Hidden Inside

by Daniel Carlton
and Nambi E. Kelley

HIDDEN INSIDE premiered with Keen Company (Jonathan Silverstein, Artistic Director) as part of the Keen Teens Festival of New Work (Celestine Rae, Festival Artistic Director) at Theatre Row in New York City on May 19, 2023. The performance was directed by Christopher Burris, with sets by Indigo Shea, costumes by Brittani Beresford, lights by Alex DeNevers, and sound by Jordana Abrenica. The Production Stage Manager was Sloane Fischer. The cast was as follows:

SLACKER	Sebastian Acosta
GOTH	Justin Rivera
JOKER	Jonathan Morales
IMMIGRANT	Cristina Lopez
VEGAN	Aicha Bathily
BULLY	Jahsiah Augúste
NEW KID	Nashmia Rahman
LONELY GIRL	Ruby Rodriguez Ronco
STUDENT TEACHER	Karla Lazala
RAPPER	Serenity Facey

CHARACTERS

SLACKER – Obsessed with stars, planets, and time.

GOTH – Socially awkward. Speaks in poetry that comes off to many as cryptic. An observer of people.

JOKER – Laughs and jokes to keep from crying.

IMMIGRANT – Woman. Recently moved from a predominantly Spanish-speaking country. She speaks English, but slip into Spanish when struggling for words.

VEGAN – Woman. Being a Vegan is an identity. She is also a secret bulimic.

BULLY – Tough exterior. Often abrasive, so that they don't seem vulnerable.

NEW KID – Recent transfer to the school. Traumatized by events that happened at their old school.

LONELY GIRL – Woman. Obsessed with being loved. Possibly pregnant.

STUDENT TEACHER – College Senior Education Major, first assignment as a Student Teacher. Often feels overwhelmed by all of the challenges that come with being a student in debt.

RAPPER – Loves to rap in both old school and modern styles. They are always testing out raps in every situation.

Note: All characters use they/them pronouns unless specifically indentified by gender.

SETTING

A small supply room, Every City, USA.

TIME

Now.

SPANISH TRANSLATION INDEX

Tarde – Late

Escóndete – Hide yourself

Sí aburrida – Yes boring

Ahora no puedo llamar a mi trabajo. – Now I can't call my work (job).

Siéntate y cállate. – Sit down and be quiet.

Cállate la boca. – Shut your mouth.

Tengo sueño. – I'm sleepy.

Ojos – Eyes

Pásalo – Pass it on

Encontré a mi gente – I found my people (my tribe).

Scene One

(An alarm clock rings.)

(Lights rise on each scattered throughout the audience in their respective homes.)

SLACKER. Gotta go, Mom, running late to Saturday school –!

LONELY GIRL. Late –!

JOKER. Gonna be late –!

IMMIGRANT. ¡Tarde –!

VEGAN. Late –!

BULLY. Late!

NEW KID. Me? Late?

GOTH. Late.

RAPPER. Uh oh! The bell for Saturday school is about to –

(Riiiiinng!)

STUDENT TEACHER. Okay late comers! Come in off the playground! Hurry up those steps and get into Saturday school, my first assignment as a student teacher! My name is –

BULLY. Teacher, don't nobody care what your name is.

STUDENT TEACHER. ...Ohhhkaaaay – Fine. Call me... Teacher.

JOKER. Just don't call 'em late for Saturday School. Get it? Late for –

(No one laughs. It ain't funny.)

JOKER. Oh never mind.

STUDENT TEACHER. Class, you know the drill. Before I let you into the school, empty them pockets. Phones in the Phone Jail Jar, you'll get them back from the security guard at the end of the day.

BULLY. What about your phone?

STUDENT TEACHER. Ah! Lead by example. Good teaching tool. Thanks.

> *(The **STUDENT TEACHER** puts their phone in the jar, and collects the other phones as the kids enter the school, all eyeballing each other.)*
>
> *(Lights.)*
>
> *(We hear their inner thoughts.)*

They think I'm failing them.

SLACKER. They think I'm failing gym.

LONELY GIRL. They think I'm failing life.

JOKER. They think I'm not funny.

IMMIGRANT. They think I talk funny.

VEGAN. They think I eat funny.

BULLY. They think I beat up anyone who looks at me funny.

NEW KID. I'm scared what they think cuz I ain't met them yet.

GOTH. I have met them and they think cuz I dress in black that I'm a freak.

RAPPER.
 THEY THINK I GET STACKS
 SACKS

AND RACKS
LIKE STRAHAN USED TO GET QUARTERBACKS
MY RAP ATTACK.
MAKES EVERYBODY STEP BACK
BACK
BACK
CHECK THE TRACK
I'M THE TRUTH
TRUTH
TRUTH
SPEAK FOR THE FLY YOUTH
DON'T NEED NO BOOTH
THEY WHACK ANALOG
I'M BLUETOOTH
STARS, STARS, STARS
NO CAP BARS

> *(The **STUDENT TEACHER** collects the last phone as –)*

> *(Lights.)*

STUDENT TEACHER. Excellent. You, take these phones to the security guard and come right back.

RAPPER. Copy!
LIKE A BLAST
BE BACK FAST
IN A FLASH

> *(They exit.)*

STUDENT TEACHER. Now. Saturday school is a make-up day. We are doing things you missed because you all were chronically late. So, first up...

(Reading from notes.) ...An active shooter drill in the supply room?

> *(The **STUDENTS** groan.)*

BULLY. That small room?

LONELY GIRL. Makes me feel claustrophobic.

JOKER. Smells like feet in there.

STUDENT TEACHER. Hey, hey now. WE can do this. Leave your backpacks, water bottles, everything. Single file down the hallway into the supply room, now.

> *(The **STUDENTS** all single-file line into the supply room as **RAPPER** rejoins.)*

RAPPER. Damn it's tight in here.
DON'T NOBODY TOUCH ME HERE
ALL Y'ALL KEEP CLEAR

STUDENT TEACHER. Good, you're back. Okay now. Let's go!

> *(Riiiiingg! Riiiiingg!!! **TEACHER** rings the panic alarm. It sounds like the end of the world.)*

Scene Two

(As the alarm continues... **TEACHER** *reads the lesson plan...)*

STUDENT TEACHER. This is a drill! I repeat, this is a drill! You all know what to do, let's go.

(The **STUDENTS** *prep the room for lockdown.)*

LONELY GIRL. Turn off the lights.

SLACKER. Lock the doors.

VEGAN. Cover the windows.

IMMIGRANT. Stay away from the windows.

JOKER. Turn off your phones –

LONELY GIRL. If we had phones that is –

VEGAN. Huddle together –

BULLY. In the corner furthest from the door –

STUDENT TEACHER. But on the same wall as the door –

BULLY. So we won't be seen, we know, we know.

NEW KID. Be quiet.

GOTH. And hide.

RAPPER. Hide.

SLACKER. Hide.

LONELY GIRL. Hide.

JOKER. Hide?

IMMIGRANT. ¡Escóndete!

VEGAN. Hide.

BULLY. Hide!

STUDENT TEACHER. Hide. Good. Now.

SHHHHHHHHHHHhhhhhhhh...

> *(The **STUDENTS** are quiet for an eternity. They all eye each other, cautious.)*

> *(Lights.)*

> *(Inner thoughts.)*

BULLY. This is boring.

IMMIGRANT. Sí, aburrida.

SLACKER. It's dumb.

LONELY GIRL. It's scary!

JOKER. Where's the joke?

VEGAN. Where's the food?

BULLY. Where's the shooter? I'll kick his –

NEW KID. This is depressive!

GOTH. Oppressive!

RAPPER. To me, see it's progressive.

LONELY GIRL. Progressive?! No, no, this quiet, it's –!

> *(Lights.)*

> *(**LONELY GIRL** starts heaving uncontrollably.)*

SLACKER. Uh oh.

STUDENT TEACHER. What's wrong?

LONELY GIRL. P-P-P-anic attttaccccckkkkk –!

VEGAN. I get those too when I eat too much –

NEW KID. Me too when I have to figure out people –

LONELY GIRL. I-I-I-I can't can't can't – breeeeeeathe!

NEW KID. I seen this at my old school. Teacher, end the drill!

STUDENT TEACHER. Okay, okay –!

> (*The **TEACHER** rings a bell ending the drill. **LONELY GIRL** calms.*)

JOKER. Whew! Dodged a bullet there! …Funny?

> (*Everyone scowls at **JOKER**.*)

Well, can't blame me for trying.

STUDENT TEACHER. Whew. Alright everyone. Impressive work. Especially you, new kid.

NEW KID. What if this was real? You never know who's who.

> (***NEW KID** eyes everyone, they all feel their gaze and it doesn't feel good.*)

STUDENT TEACHER. …Okay, yeah, well… Let's restore the room now.

(*To **LONELY GIRL**.*) You good?

LONELY GIRL. Just need some water.

BULLY. All our water bottles are in the classroom, teacher.

STUDENT TEACHER. Okay then, back to the classroom, let's go. Single-file line, please.

> (*They line up, getting to the door. It's locked.*)

Who locked the door?

SLACKER. I did.

STUDENT TEACHER. So unlock it.

SLACKER. You didn't give me a key.

STUDENT TEACHER. Of course I did.

SLACKER. Look. Just because my grades are whack and I stare at the stars all night doesn't mean I'm dumb. I was NOT given a key.

STUDENT TEACHER. I did!

ALL. You didn't!

STUDENT TEACHER. ...Okay, no problem! I'll just...call the guard.

BULLY. But Teacher...you don't got your phone.

STUDENT TEACHER. ...Okay, okay... We will ring the P.A. system to the office. Problem solved.

> (**STUDENT TEACHER** *pushes the button multiple times. But...*)

Broken. Okay... Does anyone have a laptop? iPad, Apple Watch? Burner phone?

BULLY. Burner phone? We ain't drug dealers on a TV show in the 90s.

STUDENT TEACHER. ...Okay then. Everyone just...bang on the door. Now!

> (*They all do. No security guard.*)

Okay... Bang AND yell.

> (*They all do. No security guard.*)

Okay... WHERE'S THE SECURITY GUARD?!

RAPPER. The game.

STUDENT TEACHER. Game? What game?!

RAPPER. The Metropolis Colts. Said he was leaving early since we were a small group.

STUDENT TEACHER. Is he coming back?

RAPPER. Proposing to his dude on the Kiss Cam at halftime. So...no?

SLACKER. Just get 'em fired.

BULLY. Yeah, we go through guards like dirty draws at this school.

   (The **STUDENT TEACHER** *sits, devastated.)*

SLACKER. Teacher... You crying?

Scene Three

*(Everyone retreats to separate corners as the **TEACHER** consults their notes.)*

STUDENT TEACHER. Okay, quiet. Sit still while I figure out what to do.

BULLY. It stank in here.

JOKER. That funk is you, no joke.

NEW KID. All o' you stay away from me.

JOKER. Smell like onions.

VEGAN. I ain't got no onion nothin' in my bag.

LONELY GIRL. Damn why you bump me?!

RAPPER. Ain't bump you, I'm way over here.

LONELY GIRL. Stay out my sunlight!

BULLY. What you lookin' at, new kid?

NEW KID. I'll let you know *if* we get out o' here.

SLACKER. *If?* I don't feel good.

STUDENT TEACHER. What's wrong with you?

SLACKER. Mercury's in retrograde. It's literally spinning backwards in its orbit. Now I gotta deal with this?

NEW KID. This is my first day here. Well, my make-up first day. Cuz I missed the first *first* day. Could be all of our last.

JOKER. Damn girl, how many first first days you got?

VEGAN. The way this is going it might be our last! Pass the vegan Takis.

BULLY. Excuse me, weird kid who eats weird food! Don't talk like that! It's making everybody sick. I'm sick of listening to you already.

IMMIGRANT. What's weird about Takis? I love Takis? With a little hot chili and lime?

VEGAN. Oooh, gotta try that. Especially since it's vegan –

BULLY. WEIRD!

STUDENT TEACHER. That's enough! You all need to treat each other with respect. Now, anybody have a medical problem? My notes say that in these situations, statistics tell us –

BULLY. Yo, too many big words! You ain't no docta, speak English.

IMMIGRANT. I DO speak English!

BULLY. I ain't talking to you. And if I was, you'd know it, so don't mess up my lucky day.

SLACKER. Lucky day? What's lucky about Mercury in retrograde?

BULLY. Lucky day. Cuz we get to chill all day.

(*To* **RAPPER**.) Yo, spit some words for the occasion, Fake Drake.

RAPPER. I'm good like a street ball in the hood.
SNIPERS SHOOT UP SCHOOLS LIKE HATERS
I'M AN UNTOUCHABLE PIMP WITH JORDAN GATORS
MY RHYME FLOW KILLS
STRESS YOU LIKE A CELL PHONE BILL
I'M NOT SAYING I'M GREAT
STOP, DROP, AND APPRECIATE
CUT YOURSELF A SLICE
I BAKE THE WHOLE CAKE
CUZ FAKE DRAKE, I AIN'T

IMMIGRANT. Fake Drake? Who's Drake again?

SLACKER. He's only sold 170 ka-trillion records.

NEW KID. How do you know all that?

SLACKER. Why? You watchin' me too? I may be a slacker, but I'm good at some things. Like, time. We've been in here exactly –

(**SLACKER** *flips open the shade and looks at the sun.*)

eleven minutes and fifteen seconds.

(They all collectively groan.)

LONELY GIRL. Teacher? How much longer? I feel nauseous.

NEW KID. Teacher! This girl is sick. What's your book say to do now?

BULLY. Old girl is sick? Ha! You ain't got this, bruh.

STUDENT TEACHER. Don't bully me. I'm not a kid. Graduating college this year.

VEGAN. Graduating college? So old. Look like a baby to me though. So skinny.

LONELY GIRL. I need to call my mom.

BULLY. Our phones are in the Jail Jar. With the security guard! Remember?

JOKER. Phone Lives Matter?!

(Looks around, no one thinks it's funny.)

Dayum. Y'all gon' laugh today.

IMMIGRANT. I have to get to work today! Ahora no puedo llamar a mi trabajo.

NEW KID. Call your job? A job as a cover. So it *could* be you –

IMMIGRANT. *What* could be me?

BULLY. Yo, New Kid is whack.

IMMIGRANT. And I got two jobs. Babysit too.

VEGAN. That's probably why you're so slim. When I'm a movie star model, I need to keep my body and my look tight.

NEW KID. You look alright to me.

BULLY. Cuz you know that new kid's watchin' all o' us!

VEGAN. Aw, leave 'em alone!

BULLY. Or what?

STUDENT TEACHER. Easy, Kids.

LONELY GIRL. I have to call my man. He must be going crazy right now worrying about me. I haven't text him in like, fifteen minutes.

SLACKER. Actually seventeen minutes and eighteen seconds –

VEGAN. How you know what time it is?

NEW KID. Haven't you seen him watching the sun? The modern clock is based on the ancient sundial.

SLACKER. Yeah. Keep up.

JOKER. Can't tell time on an old clock. Only on a digital one. Like my phone.

(Everyone laughs.)

That's not a joke.

(Oops.)

LONELY GIRL. Whatever time it is I still need to call my mom.

BULLY. "I have to call my mom." "I have to call my man." Damn, girl, can't you be alone?

RAPPER. Yeah, that bootleg man is probably glad that you can't call. This way he can go see his other birds.

JOKER. One thing about birds, they all think that they have the only nest. Here **chickie chickie**!

(They laugh.)

LONELY GIRL. How y'all coming out of your mouth at me?!

SLACKER. I think that they are!

BULLY. Shut up, instigating fo' I pop you one!

STUDENT TEACHER. NAP ANYONE?

BULLY. Now we in kindergarten?!

NEW KID. TEACHER! Why don't you just tell that bully to shut up? You have to toughen up with kids these days. No capping allowed.

BULLY. Stand back, New Kid. This ain't whatever Disneyland school you come from.

NEW KID. What you say?! I ain't that teacher, you don't know nothin' bout me and I ain't telling you. But I will fight you –!

STUDENT TEACHER. Hey! Kids, stop, STOP –!

(Arguing ensues as...)

Scene Four

*(The **GOTH** who has been silent and alone during this time steps forward. The rest of the **STUDENTS** continue their arguments silently as **GOTH** watches, sharing inner thoughts...)*

GOTH. High School is a real haunted house. How many of us play the fool, in this social game of cat and mouse? Alone in a crowd, wishing that someone really knew your name. Instead, students chase popularity like moths to a flame. In this year, you might be out the next. Have no fear. Everybody fails that test. Failing grades is not kids' only worst fear. It's also getting dressed in the morning, hoping that they picked the right thing to wear. But people call me a freak? They see me dressed in black. That don't make me weird, weak, or a potential threat. Disdain is my attack. If we could only see inside, what are the things we are trying to hide?

*(**STUDENTS** arguing crescendos.)*

Scene Five

STUDENT TEACHER. EVERYONE QUIET!

> *(The **STUDENTS** ignore the **STUDENT TEACHER**.)*

IMMIGRANT. *(Sit down and be quiet!)* ¡Siéntate y cállate!

BULLY. You not even from here. You don't know how it is.

IMMIGRANT. You don't know what I know.

NEW KID. Always pickin' on folks as a cover. Maybe it's you.

BULLY. Maybe what's me? You really wanna fight, huh?

JOKER. Why you always messing with somebody? You act like your "you know what" don't stink. Isn't that funny? Get it? Instead of saying –

SLACKER. Don't nobody care about your jokes.

JOKER. You don't care about anything, from what I hear.

BULLY. Ouch! Yo, I wouldn't let nobody dis me like that. At my old school, I had to hurt some folks for talking out their mouths to me like that.

STUDENT TEACHER. Nobody is getting hurt. Everybody chill.

BULLY. Or what?!

VEGAN. I'm hungry.

SLACKER. Cuz it's…almost lunch time.

LONELY GIRL. Me too. But I can't keep any food down lately.

> *(**VEGAN** scans **LONELY GIRL**'s body as they do everyone, detecting a tummy bulge.)*

VEGAN. I got the fupa too. But yours looks different –

JOKER. I got jokes, but what is a fupa?

BULLY. Damn, Joker. It's the fat at the bottom of your belly. TikTok much?

STUDENT TEACHER. Is anybody else hungry?

BULLY. Teacher, we can't bring food to Saturday school.

JOKER. Can we order Grubhub? Uber Eats? My treat.

> *(Everyone stares at the **JOKER**: "Like Really?")*

Oh my God, everyone is taking my jokes seriously.

BULLY. I'm sick of hearing all of your bad jokes!

SLACKER. Me too! This is like, the worst.

VEGAN. When do we eat? This is ridiculous. What time is it now?

SLACKER. Thirty minutes more from the last time you asked.

> *(They all groan.)*

VEGAN. Wake me up for dessert. No butter.

SLACKER. It's not dessert time yet, but another hour and forty minutes has just gone by.

> *(They all groan again.)*

VEGAN. Wait? How is that possible when I just asked you two seconds ago?

SLACKER. Time moves on its own accord in... *The Twilight Zone.*

BULLY. Jordan Peele you ain't.

SLACKER. But Rod Serling I am. Old school, baby!

> *(**SLACKER** tries to remember* The Twilight Zone *theme song but...)*

I don't remember the theme song.

LONELY GIRL. I still don't feel so good.

SLACKER. Me neither.

VEGAN. Me neither.

STUDENT TEACHER. Everyone quit moving around and sit down.

VEGAN. Got something better.

> (**VEGAN** *reaches in their bag and pulls out...*)

NEW KID. (*Thinking* **VEGAN** *is pulling out a gun.*) Oh no! Everybody run, hide –!

VEGAN. Run and hide? No, new kid. It's a BAAAAGELLLL!!!

JOKER. I KNEW I SMELLED ONIONS!

> (*Everyone scrambles for the bagel as...*)

Scene Six

(The bagel fight continues upstage.)

RAPPER. You don't say much. You all right?

GOTH. Dark clouds inside skyless land with a ceiling instead of a sun. Hoodie Shrouds Decency on the run. When do we stop this fight? This struggle for the light?

RAPPER. So what are you, like, a rapper? Yo, I write a little something something myself. Wanna hear?

GOTH. ...No.

Scene Seven

(As the bagel fight continues...)

BULLY. Mine!

VEGAN. Mine!

BULLY. Mine!

VEGAN. MINE!

LONELY GIRL. We're all going to rot in here!

> *(The **LONELY GIRL**, no longer able to contain her sickness, faints.)*

STUDENT TEACHER. We've got a medical emergency!

> *(Everyone gathers around the **LONELY GIRL**.)*

Oh my God! This is serious. Now! Everyone! Back up and let her breathe!

NEW KID. Do you know first aid?

STUDENT TEACHER. Uh...well... Next semester I will.

VEGAN. We're all gonna die!

NEW KID. I know CPR! Learned it at my old school after...

BULLY. After what?

SLACKER. Why are we still here?!

RAPPER.
DOOMSDAY.
TIME TO PRAY.
WE WON'T SEE ANOTHER DAY.

JOKER. That's not funny. Now that girl is all passed out on the floor like she was posing for that old show *Top Model*. Uh... Is that funny?

VEGAN. Why don't you just shut up! Can't y'all see that fupa ain't no fupa. This girl is pregnant.

HIDDEN INSIDE

(Various oohs and aahs. Everyone is shocked. **BULLY** *rises to defend* **LONELY GIRL**.*)*

BULLY. *(To* **VEGAN**.*)* How's your stomach? I don't see no fupa.

VEGAN. What's that supposed to mean?

BULLY. Don't try to act brand new. Talkin' 'bout tofu this and gluten free that with a secret stash of onion bagels. You're not really vegan, are you? More like you gonna stick your paw down your throat and vomit all over us!

VEGAN. You want to step to me?! I'm small but mighty! And I know Kung Fu!

(She does a move.)

BULLY. Go Bruce Lee on me?!

*(***BULLY*** does a move and war cry.)*

LONELY GIRL. Stop it all of you!

*(***TEACHER*** goes to* **LONELY GIRL**.*)*

STUDENT TEACHER. Are you okay?

LONELY GIRL. Yeah. I'm okay. And…it's true. We're gonna have a baby.

(The **STUDENTS** *are silenced by the news.)*

RAPPER. "We?" How you know your dude's not fronting? The one you need to call every other minute?

LONELY GIRL. My dude?

RAPPER. Yeah. Why are you with a dude in his twenties? What he want with a girl our age?

LONELY GIRL. Why you all up in my business? You don't know me or him like that!

RAPPER. I know that dude. And I'm sorry to be the one to tell you… You ain't the only one.

LONELY GIRL. What?! Leave Me Alone!

(She covers her face, covering tears.)

SLACKER. Hey girl...you crying?

BULLY. Why you making old girl cry?

SLACKER. You bully!

BULLY. Slacker!

LONELY GIRL. Vegan!

VEGAN. Lonely girl!

STUDENT TEACHER. Cut it out, y'all!

NEW KID. Then get control, Student Teacher!

IMMIGRANT. ¡Cállate la boca *(Shut up.)*, New Kid!

JOKER. Immigrant!

RAPPER. Joker!

GOTH. Leave *them* alone, Rapper!

RAPPER. You do talk, just not to me! Goth!

> *(The **BULLY** pushes **THE RAPPER**. **VEGAN** jumps in to defend **THE RAPPER**. Soon all the tensions break, and everyone is fighting everyone as **THE GOTH** watches it all unfold.)*

VEGAN. Don't push them!

RAPPER. Get yo' hand off me –!

IMMIGRANT. Leggo my hair!

SLACKER. Why you pullin' my shirt!

BULLY. Get yo' hand out my pocket!

JOKER. Ow ow ow! Leggo my eggo!

> *(The **STUDENT TEACHER** tries to break everyone up.)*

STUDENT TEACHER. Nobody is fighting here today! STOP IT! RIGHT NOW.

(Everyone reluctantly, stops.)

I want everyone, right now, to say whatever is in their hearts. No more keeping stuff hidden inside as we are hidden inside. Right now. Say it.

(Silence.)

Lead by example... I'll start... I didn't get training for this. How am I supposed to take care of you kids, make you feel safe? I have to show you that I'm alright. I can't lose it. You have to see that I, the adult, who is not much older than you, has the upper hand. I've got things to worry about my damn self. I want to graduate from this college that I can't even afford. I can barely keep a roof over my head on this meager salary. But when I graduate, I am going to be the best teacher so that my students will see that life is not worthless. You will see that love is alive in me. Find the love in the room. Pass it on.

*(Puts hand on **JOKER**'s shoulder.)*

JOKER. Why you touching me?

STUDENT TEACHER. I'm passing it on. Passing on love. Truth.

JOKER. Oh, I got it! Copy.

*(The **JOKER** accepts being touched and then...)*

I like making people laugh. They laugh with you, or they laugh at you. Nobody's going to laugh at me! My life ain't that funny anyway. My auntie got the big C, you know? When I leave here, if I leave here, I got to drive her to the doc where they pump that stuff in her to make her better. Seem to me it just make her sicker.

Then I drive her home. Order Grubhub and feed her. Wash her with that purple soap she like, if she let me. Cuz she's all I got, you know? Everyday I hope that I don't get that call. You know, the one that says she... I laugh to keep from crying. Pretty funny huh? ...Pass it on.

> (**JOKER** *puts their hands on* **IMMIGRANT***'s shoulder.*)

IMMIGRANT. You try working and going to school. You try learning another language. Do you know that I think in Spanish and talk in English? I have to translate in my head all of the time. You try babysitting other people's kids when you just want to be a kid too. Do you help to pay the bills in your house? I do in mine. Mami's working two shifts and Papi's barely home. The little one's can't help. Tengo sueño, I can't even keep my ojos open. I can't think of anything else. Psh, what am I gonna do? Es verdad, life is hard for people not from here. Pásalo.

> (**IMMIGRANT** *puts their hand on* **VEGAN***'s shoulder.*)

VEGAN. My hands grip the edge of the seat. Slipping off my hot and sweaty palms. Brush the strands of my hair off of my blood red cheeks. I can't hold it anymore. The burning sensation is starting to begin. I can feel the acid burning my flesh layer by layer. I can't stop it now. It has a mind of its own. And then my mouth is open, gagging and hurling, I can feel the hot tears stroll down my face. For once I'm in control. Pass it.

> (**VEGAN** *puts their hand on* **NEW KID***'s shoulder.*)

NEW KID. I was always late at my last school too. You know why? 'Cause Valentine's Day of my freshman year, like every other day, I was on time. And this kid in my algebra class walked right by me, took out a weapon, and started... After that, I vowed then I won't never be on time to school ever again. And the school flunked me out! Like I did something wrong for being scared. How do you know if you got PTSD if nobody even talks to you about it? They just shove you off, make you the new school's problem. And now I'm here. But you all feel that fear too. I seen it in all your eyes when Teacher started the drill. You looked around and wondered, if this was real, could it be one of us? Could it be you? You? Or even me, the new kid? That's why I clock everyone, check every entrance, exit, and form an escape plan in my mind. And I won't feel safe until I do cause that's the messed up reality of what we living right now. Every. Damn. Day... Who's left?

*(**NEW KID** puts their hand on **LONELY GIRL**'s shoulder.)*

LONELY GIRL. I'm an only child. And I loved playing with dolls growing up cuz I ain't had no brothers or sisters to play with. My dolls kept me from feeling alone. Now I'ma have a real live doll. I'ma have this baby. And since I'm about to be a parent, I can imagine I will care and fear for this baby more than I have words to share. My loneliness was about me. But being a parent ain't about me. It's about my baby. And having a task, someone to care for outside of me gives me purpose. And that fills me. This world ain't pretty. But I'ma do it. I'ma keep it. And protect her with all I got. Pass.

*(**LONELY GIRL** puts her hand on **BULLY**'s shoulder.)*

BULLY. ...I wish that I wasn't such a prisoner. My jail cell is my mind. Free Me! In the first grade somebody said, "You don't color right." Then they said, "You don't know your ABC's because you're stupid." In fifth grade they started to hate on me. In High School, I'm a star. This is my school. Who's stupid now? I make people think what I want them to think about me. No, that's not right. Mean is one thing that I don't want to be. I hope everyone can forgive me, and see me not for what I'm trying to be. See me for me... Pass it on.

*(**BULLY** puts hand on **SLACKER**'s shoulder.)*

SLACKER. I like to dance and be anything but me. But my body gets worn out so fast. I act the way that I act because I feel like a prisoner too. Not in my mind, but in my body. The real me is not what you see. I have an immunodeficiency. Yeah my grades suck and when I get tired, I do give up. But right now I hope that you can see that I'm showing you the actual me. Pass it.

*(**SLACKER** puts hand on **RAPPER**'s shoulder.)*

RAPPER.

Frustration in my mind as time goes by

Thinking what am I going to do with myself I need help I've

Been discriminated and hated. Now I've got to face it.

Talk to the Lord. He's my world. But what use is He?

When people still abusing me? Why can't I just be

free? Man, when will my life ever get any better?

TRAPPED WITH MY PEERS

PEERS

PEERS

MOST OF US SCARED TO DROP TEARS

TEARS

TEARS

EVEN THOUGH WE FEEL LOST HERE

HERE

HERE

WE AIN'T GOING NOWHERE.

NOWHERE

NOWHERE

KEEP OUR HEADS CLEAR

CLEAR

CLEAR
COULD HELP BE NEAR?
NEAR?
NEAR?
NOT JUST IN MY RHYME FLOW
FLOW
FLOW
IT'S TIME TO KNOW
KNOW
KNOW
WHICH DIRECTION TO GO
GO
GO
IF PEOPLE WASN'T TRYING TO HIDE
HIDE
HIDE
TRUTH IS WHAT YOU'D SEE INSIDE
INSIDE
INSIDE
PASS IT
PASS IT
PASS IT
PAIN, GOTTA OUTLAST IT.
OUTLAST IT
OUTLAST IT

> (**RAPPER** *puts their hand on* **GOTH**'s *shoulder.*
> **GOTH** *hesitates as everyone watches.*)

GOTH. I say to my mother, "Stop! Stop! I'm not taking this anymore. You let him come in here, and he'll hurt you over and over again. You say that you love him and can't leave him to the streets, but when he leaves you, the pills are your only pain reliever. But what about me huh? Am I not enough for you to leave the drugs alone? Am I not enough for you to see that you're not the only one in pain? Am I enough for you at all?" …I can't breathe.

*(The **GOTH** crumbles. Everyone circles **GOTH**, gently putting their hands on them to calm them, a laying on of hands. The teens all hold each other as **GOTH** speaks what they all feel inside.)*

GOTH. ...I'm scared.

SLACKER. ...Me too.

LONELY GIRL. Me too.

JOKER. Yup.

IMMIGRANT. Terrified.

VEGAN. So scared.

NEW KID. Me too.

RAPPER. Me too.

BULLY. ...Alright. Me too.

*(Everyone breathes and sways together gently, a healing circle of hands. The **STUDENT TEACHER** smiles, proud.)*

SLACKER. ...What's your name?

*(The **STUDENTS** each share their names [insert real actor's names], with the **STUDENT TEACHER** sharing their name last.)*

VEGAN. What time is it now?

SLACKER. Evening. Venus is rising. See? Look at her, over the horizon, on the other side of the setting sun...

(As they all gaze at beautiful Venus in this poignant, perfect moment...)

LONELY GIRL. Thanks for telling me about my so-called man. The truth hurts, but I have to live with it.

RAPPER. What you gonna do?

LONELY GIRL. Gonna talk to my mother. I know that she's gonna flip on the news, but the truth is the truth.

VEGAN. I'll go with you if you need me to.

> *(The **GOTH** walks over. It's the first time they have engaged anyone the whole time.)*

GOTH. ...Could you use another friend?

RAPPER. Oh snap!

VEGAN. Wait. Who are you talking to?

GOTH. All of you. I judged you all too much.

NEW KID. I ain't gon' front, I thought if anybody was a shooter, it was probably you.

LONELY GIRL. Maybe we all judge each other too much.

VEGAN. And we hide from ourselves too.

JOKER. Not me!

> *(They all stare at the **JOKER**.)*

Just jokes!

> *(They all laugh at the **JOKER** for the first time.)*

STUDENT TEACHER. Now, since we are stuck in here until God knows when, we may as well continue with the lessons for today...

> *(The **STUDENTS** groan as the **TEACHER** pulls out their notes.)*

Uh oh...my bad. Guess what I just found?

> *(A key drops to the floor from inside their notepad. The **STUDENTS** heave a sigh of relief.)*

Alright, y'all. Let's get out of here.

(**TEACHER** *unlocks the door and they all head toward the exit, some hugging, patting each other on the back, now a community. As they leave, we hear their inner thoughts...*)

(Lights.)

SLACKER. I'ma push my body a little harder so I can hang with these folks who like me.

LONELY GIRL. They think I'm brave for having this baby. And I am.

VEGAN. They think I'm cute. But more importantly, *I* think I'm cute.

JOKER. They think I'm funny.

IMMIGRANT. I found my tribe.

Encontré a mi gente.

NEW KID. I found release.

RAPPER. They hear my rhyme.

BULLY. They see my truth.

STUDENT TEACHER. I'm going to be a good teacher. Yeah...

*(The **GOTH** watches, one last look.)*

GOTH.
To hesitate or face your fate,
Life is short
It doesn't wait
Never too early, or lose out when you're late.
If life is about what you do with the date,
I refuse to be left
With an empty plate

(Lights.)

*(**VEGAN** pops back in with a bag of…)*

VEGAN. Takis?

*(As the **GOTH** exits, lights fade to black.)*

Milton Keynes UK
Ingram Content Group UK Ltd.
UKHW020201300724
446181UK00014B/611

9 780573 711084